CW00855171

THE CAREER STARTER GUIDE

Finding and mastering your first job

Alan MacDonald, Tony Campolo, *etc.*

f r a m e w o r k s

FRAMEWORKS
38 De Montfort Street, Leicester LE1 7GP, England

© Alan MacDonald 1990

Unless otherwise stated, Scripture quotations in this publication are from the Holy Bible, New International Version. Copyright © 1973, 1978, 1984 International Bible Society. Published by Hodder and Stoughton.

While every effort has been made to contact the copyright holders of all extracts used in this book, the publishers have not been successful in every case. Any amendment to these acknowledgments will gladly be incorporated in future printings.

First published 1990

British Library Cataloguing in Publication Data
MacDonald, Alan, *1958*
The career starter guide : finding and mastering your first job.
1. Great Britain. Young persons. First employment
I. Title II. Campolo, Tony
331.3'4'0941

ISBN 0—85111—209—9

Set in Palacio
Typeset in Great Britain by Ian D. Grimshaw (Associates)
Printed in Great Britain by
Richard Clay Ltd, Bungay, Suffolk

Frameworks is an imprint of Inter-Varsity Press, the book-publishing division of the Universities and Colleges Christian Fellowship.

C O N T E N T S

*i*t was one o'clock in the morning when I boarded the red-eye special flight going from California to Philadelphia. I was looking forward to getting some rest, but the guy next to

me wanted to talk.

'What's your name?' he asked. And I said, 'Tony Campolo.' And then he asked, 'What do you do?'

DANGEROUS LIVING: FOLLOWING THE REAL JESUS

Now when I don't want to talk to someone I say, 'I'm a sociologist.' And they say, 'Oh, that's interesting,' and turn around. But if I really want to shut someone up, I say, 'Oh, I'm a Baptist evangelist.' Generally that floors the guy right on the spot.

So this guy asked, 'What do you do?'

'I'm a Baptist evangelist,' I said.

'Do you know what I believe?' he asked.

I could hardly wait.

'I believe that going to heaven is like going to Philadelphia.'

I certainly hope not, I thought.

'There are many ways to Philadelphia,' he continued. 'Some go by airplane. Some go by train. Some go by bus. Some drive by automobile. It doesn't make any difference how we go there. We all end up in the same place.'

'Profound,' I said, and went to sleep.

As we started descending into Philadelphia, the place was fogged in. The wind was blowing, the rain was beating on the plane, and everyone looked nervous and uptight. As we were circling in the fog, I turned toward the theological expert on my right. 'I'm certainly glad the pilot doesn't agree with your theology,' I said.

'What do you mean?' he asked.

'The people in the control booth are giving instructions to the pilot, "coming north by northwest, three degrees, you're on beam, you're on beam, don't deviate from beam." I'm glad the pilot's not saying, "There are many ways into the airport. There are many approaches we can take. There are many ways we can land this plane." I'm glad he is saying, "There's only one way we can land this plane, and I'm going to stay with it." '

n o other way

There is no other name whereby we can be saved except the name of Jesus. This Jesus who died 2,000 years ago on the cross, this Saviour who is the only way to deliver us from sin, is a resurrected Jesus. He is alive and near you this very moment. But many people are turned off to Jesus because they don't really know what he's

"...many people are turned off to Jesus..."

like. They're familiar with the *cultural* Jesus rather than the biblical Jesus.

Our society has taken Jesus and recreated him in our own cultural image. When I hear Jesus being proclaimed from the television stations across our country, from pulpits hither and yon, he comes across not as the biblical Jesus, not as the Jesus described in the Bible, but as a white Anglo-Saxon, Protestant Conservative. We have in fact done something terrible. God created us in his image, but we have decided to return the favour and create a God who is in our image. And a Jesus who incarnates what we are, rather than a Jesus who incarnates the God of eternity, is not the Jesus who can save.

"You're saying this is stupid ..."

When I was teaching in Pennsylvania, people would come to me and say, 'I don't believe in God.' The first question that I would ask them was, 'Describe to me this God you don't believe in.' They always thought that was a stupid question. But it's not. I would force them to answer it. And when they finished telling me what God is like, I would congratulate them and say, 'You're halfway to becoming a Christian, because the greatest barrier to confronting and loving the real Jesus is being confused by the cultural description of Jesus that has emerged in our society.'

Which Jesus will you follow?

You've got a decision to make. The decision is which Jesus you will choose to follow. Do you choose to follow the Jesus described in the Bible – the Jesus who died on the cross, was resurrected and still lives? Or do you choose to follow the popular Jesus who embodies and reflects our cultural values?

You say, 'What is the difference between the two?' Most important, the Jesus of the Bible differs from the cultural Jesus in what he asks of you. The biblical Jesus bids you come and give everything that you are, everything that you have to him. The biblical Jesus says, quite simply, 'Read my Scriptures. Come learn of me. And then in your everyday life, be like me.' Paul put it this way: 'Let this mind be in you, which was also in Christ Jesus.' *To be a follower of the biblical Jesus is to do exactly what the biblical Jesus would do, if he were in your circumstances.*

(Philippians 2:5, KJV)

Nothing is more controversial than to be a follower of Jesus Christ. Nothing is more dangerous than to live out the will of God in today's contemporary world. It changes your whole monetary lifestyle. People say to me, 'What do you mean! Are you suggesting that if I follow Jesus I won't be able to go out and buy a BMW?'

Let me put it quite simply: If Jesus had £20,000 and knew about kids who are suffering and dying in Haiti, what kind of car would he buy? You're saying this is stupid, this is irrelevant. No. This is where Christianity needs to be applied. You've got to buy what Jesus would buy, you've got to dress with the kind of clothes that Jesus would dress in.

There's no room for conspicuous consumption. Our culture has in fact conditioned us to want more and more stuff we don't need, so that we have become consumers of God's wealth while the hungry of the world suffer and the hungry of the world die.

It's time to repent of our affluence. Christians have lost a heart for the poor. Dr Roberta Hestenes says that you're not a Christian in the full sense of the word until your heart is broken

"Nothing is more dangerous ..."

by the things that break the heart of Jesus.

*b*roken for the poor

I often urge young adults to go to the Dominican Republic or Haiti on study tours during the month of January. The first time I took a group there was a flu epidemic. I had never seen anything like it. In this country when people get the flu, they miss school. But when people are extremely malnourished, they die from it.

As we wandered through the slums, mothers were coming out of their shacks carrying the corpses of children who had died during the night. We went to the edge of the town and dug a ditch. And into the ditch we dropped these dead kids. We looked across the ditch as the priest prayed and the mothers screamed.

Then I saw one of the group, a macho basketball player, break down. His fists were clenched. His chin was trembling. Tears were streaming down his cheeks. And I knew that his heart had been broken by the things that broke the heart of Jesus. Blessed are they that mourn.

You're saying, 'Are you suggesting that you can't be rich and follow the biblical Jesus at the same time?' Hey, I'm not the guy that dreamed up the line that it's harder for rich people to enter the kingdom of heaven than for a camel to go through the eye of a needle. That's somebody else's line. You're saying, 'You're going to insult rich people.' I say this: *'If anyone has material possessions and sees his brother in need but has no pity on him, how can the love of God be in him?'* And that's what I'm asking. Please, if this offends you, be offended.

Reject Jesus if you must, *but don't take the biblical Jesus and turn him into something that*

"*Tears were streaming down his cheeks ...*"

(1 John 3:17)

8

he is not. He is the Jesus who asks, 'Are you willing to lay it on the line?' For unless men and women deny themselves they cannot enter the kingdom of heaven.

Surrender or reverence?

It boils down to this: The biblical Jesus asks more of us than the cultural Jesus. The cultural Jesus only asks us to be reverent and religious. The biblical Jesus calls us to say, 'Jesus, I want you to take my life and use it to do something fantastic. I want you to send me to those places where you need me most. If it's Africa, it's Africa. If it's Philadelphia, it's Philadelphia. If it's Buenos Aires, it's Buenos Aires. If it's Calcutta, it's Calcutta. I'll go where you want me to because I'm yours.' The biblical Jesus wants to employ you in the place where he can use you to the optimum level.

You might ask, Why is that overseas? Why is that in the inner city? Sorry, gang, but much of the West is overstaffed. We have so many people coming out of colleges and universities these days that the middle-class society can't absorb them all. You don't have to go to work for Ford Motors. It'll survive without you. You don't even have to be a doctor in an affluent suburb. They've got enough. And you don't have to add to the supply of middle-class lawyers.

Remember on 'Star Trek' when the Starship Enterprise flung out into the darkness and the voice said, 'challenged to boldly go where no man has gone before'? That's the kind of challenge the biblical Jesus makes. To do what no-one's ever done. To be what no-one's ever been.

Sure, being a missionary is hard. But most of

"What do yuppies do, anyway?"

the alternatives are very dull. What do yuppies do, anyway? Work all week, come home, sit in the jacuzzi, and tell each other, 'This is wonderful.'

If you want to be a schoolteacher, why teach in a place where they don't really need you? Why not let God take you and place you where you are absolutely essential? If you want to be a doctor, why not go where you're desperately needed? Why would anyone want to be a doctor where many of your patients aren't even sick when you can go to a place where the life and death of hundreds of people will be depending on you daily?

You can make a difference

And if you don't think you – a young person without much experience – can make a difference in this world, you're crazy. I was asked to be a counsellor in a children's camp. Everybody ought to be a counsellor in a children's camp – just once. A kid's concept of a good time is picking on people. And in this particular case, at this particular camp, there was a little boy suffering from cerebral palsy. His name was Billy. And they picked on him.

Oh, they picked on him. As he walked across the camp with his uncoordinated body they would line up and imitate his grotesque movements. I watched him one day as he was asking for directions.'Which ... way is ... the ... craft shop?' he stammered, his mouth contorting. And the boys mimicked in that same awful stammer, 'It's ... over ... there ... Billy.' And then they laughed at him. I was irate.

But my fury reached its highest pitch when, on Thursday morning, it was Billy's cabin's turn to

" ... a little boy suffering from cerebral palsy ..."

"... five minutes to say seven words ..."

give devotions. I wondered what would happen, because they had appointed Billy to be the speaker. I knew that they just wanted to get him up there to make fun of him. As he dragged his way to the front, you could hear the giggles rolling over the crowd. It took little Billy almost five minutes to say seven words.

'Jesus ... loves ... me ... and ... I ... love ... Jesus.'

When he finished, there was dead silence. I looked over my shoulder and saw junior high boys bawling all over the place. A revival broke out in that camp after Billy's short testimony. And, as I travel all over the world, I find missionaries and preachers who say, 'Remember me? I was converted at that children's camp.' We leaders had tried everything to get those kids interested in Jesus. We even imported baseball players whose batting averages had gone up since they had started praying. But God chose not to use the superstars. He chose a kid with cerebral palsy to break the spirits of the haughty. He's that kind of God.

The biblical Jesus asks you to give yourself to him no matter what you're like and no matter what you can do or can't do. He wants to use you to do the work of the kingdom.

You may have always believed in Jesus. You may have always thought it was enough to have the right theological postulates. But if theologically agreeing with the Scriptures could get you into heaven, Satan would be saved. The Scriptures say even Satan believes and trembles.

The cultural Jesus asks you only to *believe* the right stuff. The biblical Jesus asks you to *live out* the right stuff. To believe in Jesus is to say to him, Jesus, I want to surrender to you.

tony campolo

"He's that kind of God ..."

Originally published as 'The Urgency of the Call' *in Urban Mission: God's Concern for the City*, edited by John E. Kyle. © 1988 by InterVarsity Christian Fellowship of the USA. Used by permission of InterVarsity Press, P.O. Box 1400, Downers Grove, Illinois 60515, USA.

i f the Lord were to grant you the answer to one question, what would you ask?

My guess is that it would probably relate to his will for your life as you think about your education and beyond.

Our peace and satisfaction depend on knowing that God is guiding us.

But we have a problem because we are confused about what the

TRUSTING GOD'S WILL

will of God is. Most people speak of God's will as something you have or you don't have. 'Have you discovered God's will for your life?' someone may ask you. In asking this question they usually mean, have you discovered God's *blueprint* for your life? The fact is that God seldom reveals an entire blueprint, and if you are looking for that blueprint, you are likely to be disappointed. What he does most frequently, however, is to reveal the next step to you.

TRUSTING GOD'S WILL

A sensational plus to being a Christian is knowing that God has a plan for your life. *'For we are God's workmanship, created in Christ Jesus to do good works, which God has prepared in advance for us to do.'*

(Ephesians 2:10)

And he has promised to reveal his will to us. *'Trust in the Lord with all your heart, and lean not on your own understanding; in all your ways acknowledge him and he will make your paths straight.'*

(Proverbs 3:5-6)

God's will has two sides: the side where he has already revealed exactly what he wants in his Word; and the side where he has not set down specific guidelines.

Has it ever struck you that most of God's will has already been revealed in Scripture? These are the aspects of his will which apply to every Christian. We are commanded by our Lord to go into all the world and preach the gospel to every creature. God tells us in unmistakable terms that we are not to be unequally yoked together with unbelievers. Are you praying for guidance about whether you should marry a non-Christian? Save your breath. Try making a list of all the commands that apply to you from the book of *James*. You'll have a good beginning in knowing God's will for you in many areas.

(2 Corinthians 6:14)

The late A. W. Tozer pointed out that we should never seek guidance about what God has already forbidden. Nor should we ever seek guidance in the areas where he has already said yes and given us a command. He then points out that in most things God has no preference. He really doesn't have a great preference whether you eat steak or chicken. He's not desperately concerned about whether you wear a green shirt or a blue shirt. In many areas of life, to use Tozer's phrase, God invites us to consult our own

"Save your breath ..."

sanctified preferences.

Then Tozer points out that there is, on the other hand, the second side of God's will, those areas where we need special guidance. The Lord spoke to the prophet Isaiah: *'I am the Lord your God, who teaches you what is best for you, who directs you in the way you should go.'* In these areas of life there is no specific statement like 'John Jones shalt be an engineer in Scunthorpe', or 'Thou Mary Smith shalt marry Fred Illingworth.' No verse in the Bible will give you those kind of details about your life.

(Isaiah 48:17)

By recognizing the two aspects of God's will — that which is already revealed in his Word and those areas about which it is not specific — you get away from the static concept of the blueprint. The will of God is not a package let down from heaven on a string. We can't grope after it in desperation and hope that sometime in the future we'll be able to clasp it to our hearts and know we have the will of God because we've got the magic package.

The will of God is far more like a scroll that unrolls every day. God has a will for you and me today, tomorrow and the next day and the day after that. Every one of us continues to seek the will of God throughout the whole of our lives. Now it may well be that a decision which you make will commit you for three months, or two years, or five or ten years, or a lifetime. But the fact still remains that the will of God is something to be discerned and lived out every day of our lives. It is not something to be grasped once and for all.

Because of this, our call is not basically to a plan, a blueprint, a place or a work, but our call is basically to follow the Lord Jesus Christ.

TRUSTING GOD'S WILL

Prerequisites

So what are the prerequisites for knowing the will of God in the unspecified areas of our lives? The first is *to be a child of God*. One day some people asked Jesus directly, 'What must we do to be doing the works of God?' And Jesus answered, 'The work of God is this: to believe in the one he has sent.' We must first come to the Lord Jesus Christ in a commitment of faith to him as Saviour and Lord. Then we are God's children and can be guided by him as our Father.

A second prerequisite for finding God's will is that *we need to be obeying God where we know his will*. What's the point of God guiding us in areas where he's not been specific when we're apparently unconcerned about areas where he is specific? Mark Twain wryly observed that it wasn't the parts of the Bible he didn't understand that bothered him, but the parts he did understand.

We need to begin to obey what we already know to be the will of God. We know we ought to be meeting with the Lord every day in prayer. 'But you don't know my schedule this year. I've got eighteen hours.' All of us have twenty-four hours to spend. It's a matter of setting priorities. If you're going to meet with God every day, it means you decide when you're going to bed, when you're getting up and how much time you can spend in prayer in the morning. Commit yourself to God now to do certain things you already know are his will.

The third prerequisite is that *we must be willing to accept the will of God in these unspecified areas of our lives without knowing what it is*. For most of us, I suspect, this is where the real problem lies. If we're honest, most of us

" ... knowing the will of God ..."

(John 6:29)

"Mark Twain wryly observed ... "

FIRST PRIORITIES

"Have you ever felt that?"

would have to admit that our attitude is, 'Lord, show me what your will is so I can decide whether it fits in with what I have in mind and whether I want to do it or not.'

That attitude reflects the fact that we do not trust God to know best what will work out for our lives. We don't believe that he has our good at heart. We're saying, 'I think I know better, God, what will make me happy, and I'm afraid that if I trust my life to you, you're going to shortchange me.' Have you ever felt that? It's a solemn thing to realize. We make the tragic mistake of thinking that the choice is between doing what we want to do and being happy, and doing what God wants us to do and being miserable. We think the will of God is some terrible thing that he shoves under our nose and says, 'Are you willing, are you willing?' We think that if we could just get out from under his clammy hands, we could really swing. We see God as a celestial Scrooge who leans down over the balcony of heaven trying to find anybody who's enjoying life, and says, 'Now, cut it out.'

Celestial Scrooge

Nothing could be further from the truth.

It's a slur on the character of God that those ideas even cross our minds. We need to have the tremendous truth of *Romans 8:32* deeply planted in our hearts: *'He who did not spare his own Son but gave him up for us all — how will he not also, along with him, graciously give us all things?'* If you can get hold of that verse and allow it to get hold of you, you will have solved ninety per cent of your problem about desiring the will of God. You'll realize that the God who loved you and me enough to die for us when we didn't care about

16

him is not about to shortchange us when we give our lives to him.

I have two children, a daughter, Debbie, and a son, Paul. My children come to me and say, 'Daddy, I love you.' Do I respond by saying, 'Ah, children, that's just what I've been waiting to hear. Now into the cellar for three weeks. Bread and water. I've just been waiting for you to tell me you love me so I can make your life miserable'? No. Just the opposite. They can get almost anything they want out of me at that point.

h eavenly Father

Do you think that God is any less loving than a human father? God's love so far transcends any love that we humans have that it can never be expressed. The Lord is constantly drawing contrasts between human love and our heavenly Father's love. If you being evil, he says, know how to give good gifts to your children, how much more shall your heavenly Father give the Holy Spirit when you ask him. When we come to God and say, 'I love you and I'm prepared to do your will, whatever you want me to do,' we can be sure that God rejoices and fits our lives into his pattern for us, that place where he, in his omniscience and love, knows we will fit hand and glove. He is our Creator, and knows us better than we will ever know ourselves.

As you look to your last years of education and life beyond, will you affirm God's will with confidence, joy and deep satisfaction? This is a very crucial prerequisite to knowing his will. And you won't be able to hold out any area or say, I'll go anywhere, Lord, but ...' or, I'll go and do anything, but it's got to be with so and so.'

"I love you ..."

(Luke 11:13)

Taken from *Affirming God's Will* by Paul E. Little (InterVarsity Press, USA, 1971). Used by permission of Mrs Marie Little.

Rather, say, 'Lord, you've created me and I belong to you. You loved me enough to die for me when I couldn't have cared less for you. Everything I am and have belongs to you. I'm not my own; I'm bought with a price, with your precious blood. I consciously and joyfully commit myself to you. Do with me what you choose.'

And when you come to that place, you'll be able to say in the depths of your heart with Paul, 'To me to live is Christ.'

paul little

as we think about our jobs and future career aspirations, we must be aware of how our convictions have been moulded by our culture. How many times have we heard the

CAREER IDOLATRY

apostle Paul's warning: 'Do not conform any longer to the pattern of this world' (Romans 12:2)? Did you ever notice that Paul's words

assume the believers in Rome would conform to the world?

Baptizing the yuppie mentality with a Christian vocabulary is one form of our *cultural conformity*.

The logic is simple: God calls us to excellence; we must commit ourselves to exceptional performance in our jobs, even if it means sacrifice, and we will be blessed by all the benefits of career advancement. What we have done, of course, is empty these words (excellence, sacrifice and

"Baptizing the yuppie mentality ..."

(Matthew 6:24)

(Ecclesiastes 5:10)

blessing) of their biblical content and pour in our culture's meaning. What do the Scriptures say is the type of excellence God expects from us who believe? What kind of sacrifice are we expected to make and for what reason? What constitutes a blessing in the Bible, and on whose action does it depend?

Another way we allow our culture to influence our career decisions is by thinking and living in two different worlds. Our faith is private and personal, and may in fact be evidenced by vital devotional times each day, but the rest of our lives (our careers, income tax, driving *etc.*) is separate and has different rules governing behaviour. Careerwise this 'Christian dualism' is especially apparent among those who make salary top priority despite Jesus' clear teaching that you cannot worship both God and mammon. Why does it take us so long to realize that pursuing wealth wastes our lives? The writer of *Ecclesiastes* said it best: *'Whoever loves money never has money enough; whoever loves wealth is never satisfied with his income. This too is meaningless.'* We may agree with these words, but do our career aspirations show that we do not really believe them?

Many of us who are in or preparing for the marketplace are not so crass that we are blindly going after 'loadsamoney'. Instead our idolatry takes a much more subtle form: we believe that a successful career can be the context for the faithful Christian life rather than that the faithful Christian life serves as the context for a successful career. This is a subtle but important distinction. It means that on a practical level we consider the search for a successful job as the first essential and, once it has been found, we then ask how can we work in our job as a Christian.

This distortion of truth confuses us. When we are convinced that our happiness, success, or fulfilment as a person will come from finding a 'fulfilling' job, we relegate our faith to 'Christian values' that we apply to our work behaviour (keeping us honest, dependable, hard-working). But this is all backwards. Instead of finding happiness by being a slave to Christ, we become enslaved to things that make us happy. (What can *I* get out of my job? How can *I* be happy in my work? What do *I* enjoy doing most?)

''... this is all backwards ...''

In stark contrast to popular culture, Scripture emphasizes the term *service*. Remember the fundamental commandments of God: *'Love the Lord your God with all your heart, and with all your soul, and with all your mind ... Love your neighbour as yourself.'*

(Matthew 22:37-39)

Scripture in effect changes the questions that we should be asking ourselves. Instead of first asking 'What can I get out of my job?', we ought to be asking 'In what area of service am I, as a minister of Christ, best able to bring reconciliation and wholeness to a broken world?' Asking ourselves how we can serve others demands an accurate knowledge of our own abilities. But it also demands that we are able to assess the current and anticipated needs of the people of the world.

Another trap we can fall into is wrongly understanding what our calling is, and consequently confusing our *vocation* with our *job*.

The New Testament never uses the word which we translate 'vocation' to mean an occupation or type of employment. The word is always used in a spiritual sense, in terms of our special calling to be children of God. Paul establishes this powerfully: *'And we know that in all things God works for the good of those who love him, who*

(Romans 8:28-29)

have been called according to his purpose. For those God foreknew he also predestined to be conformed to the likeness of his Son ...'

We have been called as disciples of Jesus Christ to be Christ-like. Our central meaning and identity are wrapped up in our relationship with Jesus.

Our employment is then part of our larger calling in the same way that our worship and leisure activities are. If we belong to Christ, we must serve him in every area of our lives, including our work, our worship and our recreation. But our jobs alone are not our vocation. Our vocation – to be conformed to the likeness of Christ – is all encompassing.

This biblical distinction is important because, without it, we can trap ourselves in numerous ways. By describing their job search in terms of seeking their calling, some Christians are really just developing a defence against anxiety. Using phrases like 'I have been called into politics' can be a defensive ploy. It protects one from threatening self-examination or the consequences of having made the wrong choice. Someone who says she was called by God into a certain career leaves little room for discussion. There is no personal choice (because God told me) and no anxiety (what else could I do?).

Another result of a confused understanding of 'calling' is that God has only one right choice for our careers. This can result in great anxiety (will I find the *right* career, the one God has chosen just for me?) or irresponsibility (I am waiting for God to find me a job). In the latter case, career decision-making is seen as God's responsibility, not ours. We therefore make excuses for not assessing our own abilities and interests. The process of choosing a career can become

"... worship and leisure activities ..."

mysterious and irrational; we wind up full of anxiety and doubt because our basis for choosing a job is grounded on nothing but vague internal feelings.

Scripture tells us that we are called to be disciples of Jesus Christ and worship him alone in every aspect of our lives. *That* is God's desire for us. We will properly understand a biblical perspective on work only when we preserve the word 'calling' for that usage and avoid the trap of narrowing down its meaning to apply to our job.

john bernbaum and simon steer

Taken from *Why Work?* by John A. Bernbaum and Simon Steer (Baker Book House, 1986). Used by permission of the publisher.

*i*n our culture, work has been squeezed into the confined understanding of 'occupation'. An occupation is work done for pay.

This has created some real problems in understanding our work life. Therefore we need to consider several misguided notions about work. A broader definition of work as 'purposeful

SELF-FULFILMENT OR GOD'S MISSION?

activity' is revealed in three biblical dimensions:
- *Expression*. Work expresses your abilities.
- *Provision*. Work provides for your needs.
- *Mission*. Work accomplishes God's agenda on earth.

Each dimension is God-given. Each serves a very real need. And each dimension is vitally important as you consider your career search. In fact, since expression, provision and mission all seem so crucial, you might ask, 'Is any one of the three more important than the others, and if so, which? Is the need for self-expression in my job more important than the reality of having to make a living? Should provision play second fiddle to the role of mission?'

Fortunately, there are answers to these questions, and they can be found by looking at Scripture. Remember what Jesus told his followers when they asked what dimension of work was most important. Did he say, 'Set your mind on providing for your needs before everything else, and all the rest will come to you as well'? No. Jesus told his followers: 'Seek first his kingdom and his righteousness . . .' There can be no doubt about Jesus' meaning. When it comes to considering what the most important goal should be in your work, the Christian's first priority must be God's kingdom. And within our three dimensions of work, this means setting your mind on mission first. If you truly believe that Jesus is right when he talks about putting God's kingdom ahead of everything else in life, then mission must be 'number one' in your life – and in your career.

Does this mean, then, that your needs for expression and provision are no longer important in work? Not at all. God takes all three dimensions seriously, and so should you. He wants you to see that expression, provision and mission are complementary – not competitive – elements of your work.

" ... real problems in understanding our work life ..."

(Matthew 6:33)

a conflict of culture

If you truly want to integrate the three dimensions of your work in order to fulfil God's mission, then you need to resolve a very real and obvious conflict of values.

If you conform to this culture's values in your

" ... fast-lane, high-octane life ..."

career decisions, then you'll echo the same cry of so many success-seekers in society: 'I want the money. I want the status. I just want to make it right to the top.'

Jesus Christ wants you to take a different course than the fast-lane, high-octane life that has our culture running on empty. Whether you're being called to the mission field in Burundi or to an inner-city law practice, Jesus says, 'Seek first the kingdom. Take my values of obedience, self-sacrifice, forgiveness and reconciliation. Take them into your home, your school, your work.'

What set of values do you choose to live by? This is probably the single most important question that you, as a Christian, will answer as you consider your own career future. Will you intentionally order your lifestyle around working for God's kingdom? Or will you become absorbed by the materialistic desires of your contemporary culture?

Resolving these questions in a way that's consistent with your faith will take generous amounts of thought, prayer and the wise counsel of trusted friends.

Though many verses of Scripture can guide you, one particular passage may be especially helpful. In the second chapter of his letter to the Philippians, Paul says this, *'Your attitude should be the same as that of Christ Jesus: who, being in very nature God, did not consider equality with God something to be grasped, but made himself nothing, taking the very nature of a servant, being made in human likeness. And being found in appearance as a man, he humbled himself and became obedient to death – even death on a cross!'*

As a Christian, can you simultaneously claim to follow Jesus Christ and think more highly of

(Philippians 2:5-8)

yourself than he did of himself? Integrating the three dimensions of your work around mission requires that you make career decisions in the light of God's values not those of your culture. When you are able to do this, you will no longer feel driven to earn big money or attain a big title. Instead, as a faithful servant, you'll be content to seek the reward that God reserves for those who work to fulfil his calling on earth: 'Well done, good and faithful servant.'

(Matthew 25:21)

Common imbalances

At this point, you may already know yourself well enough to say, 'Yes, I want my career to centre on God's mission. Yes, I am willing to base my career choices on godly values. But *how* can I integrate expression, provision and mission in a way that respects all three dimensions and, thereby, serves God?' Let's look at some of the common imbalances that Christians may experience in the working world.

Mission without expression or provision. Steve was a young Bible college graduate stepping into his first pastorate. He was energetic. He was committed to serving his congregation 'at all costs'. Steve was also young, and it showed.

His sense of mission was so strong that, while the members of his church experienced great spiritual and personal growth, Steve's family suffered. He sacrificed his modest salary to fund church activities. Steve even neglected nurturing his natural ability to preach in order to keep up with the multitude of endless tasks he thought the church expected of him.

The result? Within two years, Steve was out of breath. His family was out of money. And he and

''... Steve's family suffered ...''

his wife were out of patience, wondering 'What do we do now?' All because this young, energetic minister emphasized mission to the exclusion of expression and provision.

Steve is like a lot of well- meaning Christians. They become so 'totally dedicated to doing God's work' that they 'burn out'. It is neither godly nor beneficial to give yourself to mission if it means you ignore your responsibilities to your family. Provision, as we saw earlier, is not limited to finances. Steve's failure to provide for his family meant giving up time he would normally spend with his wife and children in order to attend another weekly church meeting. If you choose to marry and have a family, you should expect to integrate the need for provision into your work in such a way that allows you to meet your responsibilities at home.

"... he was rarely at home ..."

Expression without mission or provision. Brian was a professional footballer in the middle of his ninth season with a title-chasing team. Every Saturday afternoon he expressed his God-given talents by making inch-perfect passes in front of 20,000 enthusiastic fans. Brian was also throwing his salary away. He always seemed on the edge of debt. This, combined with the fact that he was rarely at home, brought his wife to the edge of suing for divorce. Brian regularly passed up chances to share his faith at local events and churches. But he never failed to show up on match day – when the league title was at stake.

Unfortunately, talent (whatever it happens to be), when divorced from a biblical integration with mission and provision, can never be the basis for a healthy work life. No Christian with Brian's tendency can hope to please God, who wants to show the Christian how his or her talent can bring great personal joy when it is expressed with his mission in mind.

Provision without expression or mission. Susan was a successful architect in Sydney. She had climbed high in her profession by creating stunning skyscrapers. After more than twenty years as head of her own firm, she was at the top of her career with nowhere to go but down. And that's exactly where she went as she began to realize that for years she had given herself to a career that took little advantage of her real love, which was painting. Although she attended church off and on, Susan felt far away from God, and even further away from really expressing herself with delicate oils, instead of the endless panes of smoked glass and cold steel girders.

''... Susan felt far away from God ...''

Most people are like Susan: They invest their lifework, talents and ultimate hopes of happiness in a job that pays the most. Christians are not immune from suffering this fate, especially when their will to serve God and their desire to see their own need for self-expression never grows. A career that's heavy in salary but light in both expression and mission is a career that's drastically unbalanced.

*S*tart here

Since you will probably provide for your financial needs through an occupation, you're likely to be asking, 'How can I seek mission first and still make ends meet?' Here are three common models:

Mission as occupation. The most straightforward way to dedicate yourself fully to mission and still earn a living is through finding occupational work in an organization dedicated to meeting God's agenda on earth.

Ministries and missions of all kinds are seeking personnel: youth ministries, outreach to schools and students, work with the unemployed or underprivileged, international relief and development organizations, Christian radio, social-action agencies and many more.

Occupation to support your mission. Paul was called to be an apostle, but he didn't want to be a financial burden to the church. So, Paul learned a trade – tentmaking. Paul was able to provide for his needs by making tents and still fulfil his mission of teaching and preaching.

Tentmaking is a term being used today to describe an important strategy in world evangelism. Thousands of Christians are working in secular jobs overseas and at home in order to fulfil their mission as witnesses for Christ. These secular jobs provide needed financial support plus, in over sixty countries worldwide, they provide the person with a visa unavailable to 'full-time missionaries'.

Using an occupation to support mission requires that you carefully define your mission before securing actual work. Why? Because all too often, if you select an occupation first, your mission will be forced into whatever time is 'left over'.

Mission in your occupation. You may work in a company that isn't dedicated to accomplishing God's objectives, but because of your strategic position in the company, you're able to further Christian goals on the job.

This happened with Joseph and David in the Old Testament. Both rose in government service

"... God's agenda on earth ..."

to positions that allowed them strategic opportunities for influencing world events. In both cases, their primary occupational task wasn't tied to their respective mission. Each man's occupational competence, when combined with his desire to achieve God's agenda on earth, allowed him to exercise mission on the job.

Whichever path you follow, it's critical that you seek your mission first, then order your occupational life around that mission.

intercristo's career kit

Reprinted from *U Magazine*, March 1988, adapted from *Career Kit* (Intercristo, 1985). Used by permission of Intercristo.

Choosing a career is a serious business, especially for Christians who want to serve God with their lives. But many carry around mistaken ideas of what it means

to follow Christ in one's career. The five most common myths are:—
Myth 1: Very few career options are suitable for Christians.

WHAT MAKES A JOB 'CHRISTIAN'? FIVE MYTHS

Some people believe God wants Christians to avoid 'secular' careers because they are 'worldly'. Certainly God has given guidelines and principles in the Bible that must inform one's career choice — for example, obey the government, do not steal, lie, murder or commit adultery. But what career fields do these guidelines eliminate other than becoming a Christian thief or a Christian prostitute?

It's not as simple as that, of course. While very few careers are inherently evil, individual jobs or companies may at times expect a person to misrepresent the truth, get round the law, or in some way contribute to larger goals that are morally questionable. But just because an accountant is asked to distort figures for the tax-man doesn't mean he or she should abandon an accounting career. A better bet is to look for another employer – one with integrity.

"... few careers are inherently evil ..."

Myth 2: The only true Christian careers are becoming a pastor, a missionary, or pursuing 'full-time Christian service'. All other careers are second class. While many Christians decide to serve God by starting churches or introducing others to the faith, people sometimes forget that these occupations, while very important, are only one part of life. The whole earth is the Lord's, and Christians are to do *everything* for the glory of God. God wants people to serve him in a multitude of arenas, not just the spiritual. In his eyes, any vocation is spiritual if it contributes to his greater purpose of 'reconciling the world to himself'. And in that sense, all Christians should pursue 'full-time Christian service' whether they're church-planting or corn-planting.

(Psalm 24:1)
(Colossians 3:17)

(Colossians 1:20)

But don't some occupations matter more than others? Don't presidents change the world more than paperboys? Yes, but in terms of the inherent worth or 'Christian-ness' of the work itself, both jobs are consistent with Christ's command to serve other people.

(John 13:12-17)

One way to consider whether a particular occupation is Christian is to ask, 'What if there weren't any?' That is, if no-one were pursuing this career, would the world be worse or better

33

off? Think about it. What if there weren't any dustbin men? Carpenters? Professional footballers? Accountants? Stockbrokers? Fashion colour analysers? Computer programmers? Champion wrestlers? Artists? The answers aren't always clear. But asking the question can help a person identify how a career may or may not further God's purposes in the world.

Myth 3: I shouldn't pursue any career unless I feel a specific call from God. The feeling of being called can be important. Without it one may lose all motivation, drive and energy to serve God meaningfully in the marketplace. Those who sense a call from God should confirm the feeling with concrete evidence that they are suited for a particular career. But those who don't feel a supernatural call need not fret: God often simply expects us to put our interests, gifts and talents to use in working out his will.

Either way, answering a few questions may help clarify whether a particular career is for you: How does this occupation fit with my personal goals and priorities? Will it tap my God-given interests and gifts and help me to become the person God wants me to be? Are the pressures and time demands so great that they'll adversely affect my relationships with God, my family, my friends? Are the requirements of this job compatible with my view of marriage (if I choose to marry)? Does it make the world a better place or contribute to that end? Do other Christians who know me well feel that this career suits me?

Myth 4: The career choices one makes during school or college are permanent and irrevocable. Studies have shown that the average adult changes careers at least twice before he or she

"Does it make the world a better place ...?"

turns sixty. Career choices made during school or college must be taken seriously, but, on the other hand, things can change – one's interests, one's family situation, the economy, the job market and so on. Any of these changes could lead to a career switch later on.

But a career change isn't the end of the world; it's possible to honour God in more than one field of work. Though some may never have to wrestle with a career-change decision, statistics indicate that most people will. Just knowing that fact should reduce some of the pressure you're feeling now.

Myth 5: All I can do to serve God in a 'secular' profession is to share my faith with colleagues.
This view assumes that faith and work are completely separate, unrelated parts of life. The biblical view is quite different: in God's eyes, work itself is an outworking of one's faith, a tangible expression of service to God and other people.

(Genesis 1:27-30)

But it's not enough to say simply that work itself is Christian. Even while on the job, one needs to ask continually, 'What does it take to make this job Christian?' The answer has more to do with one's attitude than one's job description.

First, we are to approach our jobs as though we were working for God and not just for employers. Enthusiasm, creativity, integrity and service – not greed, dishonesty or doing the absolute minimum – should mark followers of God.

(Colossians 3:23)

Second, we make our job Christian by modelling Christ's love as we relate to managers, colleagues and clients – the people who see us day to day and under pressure.

"... modelling Christ's love ..."

Third, we must evaluate how the company we work for affects society. Are its products beneficial? Are its methods fair to the poor? Do its goals promote justice? Do its by-products harm the environment? The answers may not be clear cut, but we need to weigh these and other factors as we decide whether our job is Christian or not.

Fourth, we can honour God by what we do with our salary. That first pay-cheque can bring great satisfaction. But it also brings power: power to do good by giving generously to the church and to those in need, or power to do evil by squandering God's resources on things we don't need.

Making a job or career 'Christian' demands more than leaving Bible verses on our desks or sharing our faith over coffee breaks. The actual work itself, as well as our behaviour on the job, may or may not be Christian. Our attitude can make all the difference.

dave veerman

First published as 'What makes a job Christian? Five myths' by Dave Veerman, HIS Magazine, October 1986. Used by permission of the author.

*i*n recent years, increasing numbers of people have asked 'Who am I?' Were the feelings behind the question better articulated, they would probably appear as, 'What

is my purpose? What do I have to offer the world? What am I made to do?'

It is one thing to know that God has given each of us gifts

IDENTIFYING YOUR GIFTS

and another to deal with the obvious problem of identifying those gifts. One method, however, can help people get answers to those questions by giving them insight into what gifts they have been given.

The key to unlocking this method is found in an intriguing verse from *Galatians*. There God exhorts us through the apostle Paul to pay special attention to our achievements: *'Each man should examine his own conduct for himself; then he can*

(Galatians, 6:4, NEB)

''... each person displays over and over again an entire behavioural system ...''

measure his achievement by comparing himself with himself and not with anyone else.' This verse not only affirms our individuality, but also gives us a way to understand who we are and what we have been given to give.

As suggested by the apostle Paul, you begin to find God's design for you by identifying achievements that give you a sense of joy or satisfaction when used in a particular way for certain purposes. Behind those achievements lie certain gifts and motivations. By gifts and motivations we do not merely mean talent. Talent is included, but we mean something far more fundamental. In our professional experience, evaluating thousands of individuals over twenty years, we have found that each person displays over and over again an entire behavioural system, which we call a 'motivational pattern'. We human beings are far more consistent in our thoughts, words and actions than we realize. We react to people, things and circumstances in the same way time and again.

The motivational pattern is evidence that God has designed us not as haphazard collections of possibilities, but as people with highly detailed gifts that differ from one individual to another. Those gifts emerge from the depths of our motives and determine our place in the scheme of things. As each animal and organism functions in a particular place in God's creation, so we, too, are designed for a particular role in the human community and in the world.

Let's take a look at the elements of your motivational pattern:

1. Key Motivator. Examining your enjoyable achievements will reveal a common thread tying

together all the things you do well. For conven-
ience, we identify this thread as your 'key
motivator'. Out of the apparent diversity of what
you have done, this key motivator emerges as the
single overriding and unifying factor.

For one person it may be meeting needs and
requirements; for another it may be overcoming
obstacles and persevering against difficulties. For
someone else the key motivator might be serving
and helping other people, building and
developing things, or gaining recognition,
honour and awards.

*''... what you
enjoy and are
good at ...''*

2. Certain motivated abilities. Through their
achievements, individuals show their ways of
getting things done. These include such abilities
as persuading the boss, conceiving ideas, writing
reports, negotiating and bargaining, analysing
problems, teaching children, finding a solution
and organizing work.

Examining your achievement experiences will
yield five to eight abilities that recur frequently.
Those abilities are the ones that you are
particularly motivated to use. That is, they are the
abilities both that you are able to use and that you
want to use.

One person is good at planning and building,
another at designing and creating; one is good at
investigating and bargaining, another at
experimenting and evaluating; one person is
good at speaking and motivating, another at
operating and maintaining; and so forth. In each
case, what you enjoy and are good at is a result
of how God made you. As God said when
arranging the construction of the tabernacle in
the wilderness, 'I have given to all able men
ability.' People have more abilities than
motivated abilities, but the use of the latter is their

(Exodus 31:6, RSV)

MAKING CHOICES

area of strength. Given the right context, using motivated abilities is rarely boring.

3. Certain subject matter. People get satisfaction over and over again by dealing with their favourite subject matter. Here are just a few examples of subject matters that people like:
- Numbers
- Money
- Details
- Methods and solutions
- People
- Mechanical things

Examining your achievement experiences will yield three to five subject matters that recur frequently. Those subjects reveal the content, the objects and the mechanisms with which you are motivated to work.

When you do find a job, you will attempt to shape or even distort it, consciously or unconsciously, to include your favourite subject matter. So finding work that requires or at least accommodates those subjects is critical.

4. Certain circumstances. People seek certain circumstances that they enjoy. If they cannot find them, frequently they will try to create them. Examples of what people look for include:
- Stress or competition
- Structured and defined situations
- Unstructured and fluid situations
- Specific projects with a clear beginning and end
- Problems that need solving

Some people want crusades to join or a Goliath to face before they are motivated. Others need a group situation in which to work. Some seek to do things requiring an immediate response to

"Some people want crusades to join ..."

"Others need a group situation ..."

demands. Others must have plenty of time to get their act together before they step out.

5. A certain way of relating to others. Through their achievements, people reveal a characteristic way of relating with others. By examining the achievements of a person, we can categorize the role they play in the workplace:

- Leader
- Independent worker
- Team worker
- Influencer
- Self-motivated manager

No part of your behavioural pattern is more criticial than how you are motivated to operate with people. This area of our design is the reason for so much distortion, confusion and imbalance in the body of Christ.

Scripture abounds in references to specific roles we are to fulfil in relation to one another. *'The gifts we possess differ as they are allotted to us by God's grace, and must be exercised accordingly: . . . the gift of adminstration, in administration . . . if you are a leader, exert yourself to lead.'* Just because we have demonstrated excellent performance in one role, we cannot expect to produce excellence in any role.

''... pursuing a career you love.''

(Romans 12:6-8, NEB)

t he details of your design

The various segments of the motivational pattern or design just outlined represent only a skeleton. Careful examination of your enjoyable achievements will further reveal who you are.

Each element of each part of the pattern has a particular quality. For example, a person may have an ability to teach, but mainly by demonstration rather than by lecturing. A person may work better one-to-one rather than with a group, or best manage others while staying involved in the action. Another is motivated to build things, but never makes the same thing twice. One person likes giving talks and presentations, but only after mastering the subject and carefully preparing what to say. Someone else loves to debate, particularly when he or she can improvise on the spot.

The existence of such a design may be a foreign idea to you. But it is there. And understanding it is the first step – a big one – towards identifying and pursuing a career you love.

ralph mattson

Reprinted from *U Magazine*, January 1987, and excerpted from *Finding a Job You Can Love* by Ralph Mattson and Arthur Miller (Thomas Nelson, 1982). Used by permission of the publisher.

For Gary Cross, ChemE 421 was not just another chemical engineering lab at Aston University. It was a prerequisite for the mission field. He not only needed his degree to

get an engineering job overseas, but he needed the interaction with his two lab partners – an Indian Sikh and an Orthodox Jew

WILLING TO WORK OVERSEAS?

– to get experience relating cross culturally.

Three years later Gary was again working side by side with people of other faiths – this time as a design engineer for a corporation building petrochemical plants overseas. Like Gary, thousands of professionals have answered Christ's call to make disciples of all nations by accepting jobs overseas. Formally, they may teach English or analyse economics; informally they serve as lay missionaries.

"... side by side with people of other faiths..."

(See Acts 20: 33-36;
1 Corinthians 9;
2 Thessalonians 3:6-15)

Self-supporting missionaries aren't an invention of today's global economy. Joseph began the practice as an agriculture administrator for the Egyptian pharaoh; Daniel later worked for the king of Babylon. The apostle Paul and his team supported themselves, even though Paul said they had a right to expect food and shelter from the young church. Because Paul made tents for a living, some refer to self-supporting Christians living overseas as 'tentmakers'.

'Countries are looking for expertise that they don't have,' says Ron Miller, communications director for Tentmakers International. 'Jobs in agriculture, food science, engineering, business computers or health care are most plentiful. 'Educators, particulary those who teach English as a second language, are in great demand.'

Yet simply getting a secular job overseas doesn't make you a missionary. Says Ruth Siemens, director of Global Opportunities: 'A lay missionary is not just a Christian who goes overseas, but one who is trained and capable to do crosscultural evangelism in his job and in his free time.'

*h*ow to prepare

So what does it take to prepare for this kind of crosscultural evangelism?

"So what does it take ...?"

Experience relating the gospel. While experts say that book learning about missions, cultures and theology helps, you can best prepare for overseas lay work by telling friends and colleagues about Jesus Christ before you go abroad. As they say in missionary circles: 'If you haven't done it here, you're not going to do it there.'

Gayle Thacker realizes how true that is. Since

returning home from nine months of job hunting and secretarial work in Spain, Gayle has enrolled in an evangelism training course at her church. 'If I had taken that course before, I could have done a lot more in Spain,' she says. 'I was going to share [the gospel] with a girl I drove to work with, but I never got around to it.'

Experience leading an evangelistic Bible study. Researcher Don Hamilton, who interviewed hundreds of tentmakers, found the most effective had led evangelistic Bible studies before going overseas. In some countries, your home Bible study will be your friends' only access to the Bible.

Sound motives. Hamilton also found that effective lay missionaries had one primary reason for going overseas: to make Jesus Christ known. The lure of adventure, travel and people in an exotic land alone isn't enough. Still, Gary Cross believes that the Lord turned his curiosity about different cultures into a call: 'I think the Lord probably calls us to do a lot of the things that we enjoy and international cultures and languages are areas that fascinate me. I took that fascination as confirmation of something I was to do.'

Similarly, those who feel called overseas but avoid traditional mission agencies because they don't want to raise support may need to resolve some deeper issues before they leave. 'Often people who want to be tentmakers don't want to raise support because of pride,' says one missions placement co-ordinator for a large Christian organization.

Language preparation. Says Ron Miller: 'We presume that if you are going with a missionary

''... The lure of adventure, travel and people in an exotic land ...''

heart, then you ought to learn the language even if you don't need it on the job – and usually you don't.' But Janet, who spent one year teaching English in China, says that knowing the language may not be necessary for short-term service. She remembers how a woman who spoke little English became a Christian through a friend who spoke no Chinese.

Church support. Gary and his wife weren't commissioned by a church when they left, but wish they were: 'When you're out in the field, and you're the only Christian around, it helps to know that there's someone who's praying for you constantly.'

Opportunities and obstacles. Once working overseas, you will be responsible for developing your own ministry. This may mean sharing your faith with a new friend over dinner or starting a Bible study. But if you're working sixty hours a week, off-the-job ministry will be limited – so you must make your job itself part of your ministry.

After months of frustration with his 'lack of ministry', Gary decided that his vision for serving others had to centre around his long workday: '[At first] I wasn't working hard at being a Christian on the job. But since I had to spend so much time at the office, I realized that if I was going to be effective, that was where I was going to have to get my act together.' He began to seek out colleagues who were interested in faith. And he became bolder in discussing his own faith, even though he was living in a 'closed' Muslim country. 'I had the advantage of being completely non-suspect as a missionary because I was there as technical support for a petro-

"... sharing your faith with a new friend over dinner ..."

chemical plant start-up. I felt freedom to speak my mind.'

Janet took advantage of the Christmas holidays to tell her English students in China about Jesus. She gave them stories to read written by Christians whose faith had helped them face personal crises. 'The response was really good. It wasn't really preaching, but life testimony. They could identify with the suffering.'

With these opportunities to tell others about Jesus also come obstacles. Many Christians tell of 'being watched' by their host government while working overseas. 'They (the Chinese) like to hire Christians because they know you are hard-working and conscientious,' says Janet, 'but if you do evangelistic things that are really up front, you're kind of slapping them in the face.'

Others suffer from isolation. Gary considered himself blessed to live only one hour away from a church. He and others caution not to go it alone spiritually; if you can't informally link up with a mission agency working near you, then try to work where there will be another Christian professional in town.

laura sokol urban

"Others suffer from isolation ..."

First published as *Willing to Work Overseas?* by Laura Sokol Urban, *U Magazine*, October 1987. Used by permission of the author.

IS FULL-TIME SERVICE FOR YOU?

Many newly converted Christians automatically assume that God wants them to abandon the career they'd trained for and work with a Christian organization. It seems the natural decision for the really committed. But if this were the case then huge areas of society would remain unsalted by a Christian presence. There is also the notion that it will somehow be easier in the Christian world. In reality, employment in Christian mission of any kind involves costs which need to be counted:

1. It is likely to be on a low wage (if not pocket money) basis.

2. It will probably mean working long hours, including evenings or sometimes weekends without overtime.

3. Your faith being part of your work can mean you are tempted to adopt a 'professional' attitude to prayer, Bible study, etc.

Set these against the advantages:

1. Your work may teach you a great deal about evangelism, studying God's word, prayer, etc.

2. You have the support and understanding of other Christians around you.

3. You are working towards goals that you can fully commit yourself to.

The question for each of us is not 'Should I go into full-time service?' but, 'Where does God want me to serve him full-time?' There are many Christian agencies needing workers, equally there are many secular professions needing Christians.

Whichever you choose, God wants you to serve him 100% with your skills, your personality and your witness in the work you do. Every Christian is a full-time Christian and the only true guideline is to follow God's leading in your life.

*m*any people think a CV is a French car until they are launched unprepared into the competitive world of job hunting. Then the CV (*Curriculum Vitae* to Latin scholars) can

become a life-saver. It will not guarantee you a job but without it you will find it hard to get a job.

But how do you go about drafting a good

WRITING A CV THAT WORKS

CV or résumé? There are no absolute rules or magic ingredients but some simple guidelines will help you to have the best chance of securing an interview with an employer.

When is a CV necessary?

The simple answer is when a job requires one. Some jobs send application forms that cover every question from your date of birth to your

Aunt Mildred's middle name. In this case it is obviously not necessary to include a CV but other jobs, however, will ask for a written application along with a CV. The CV's second use is to send speculatively to a company you are interested in working for. Thirdly, a good CV will be invaluable to you, personally, in completing application forms.

What's the point of it?

A CV is effectively a written advert aimed at promoting you to potential employers. It should give all the relevant information about you in a concise, readable form. Like the best trailers at the cinema, it should leave the customer wanting to see the whole film − or, in this case, to meet you in person.

Principles

Generally speaking your CV should be:

Short and sweet: Not more than two sides of A4 at the most. Remember the employer may have a hundred to wade through and massive amounts of information will shred his nerves and possibly your application.

Good-looking: Grubby, badly photocopied or poorly laid-out information will say something about its sender. Take time and trouble over organizing the information under headings with plenty of space between paragraphs. Use of underlined capitals will pick out key headings and phrases. From your master copy, get a stock professionally photocopied on white, grey or beige paper (bright colours may attract attention but don't inspire confidence).

A common mistake is to spend too much time on your history and interests and too little on the employer's needs and expectations. Try to gauge what will interest an employer in the field you are in.

Job-centred: Every job is different, and although a CV is designed to be a versatile document, it may sometimes be worth tailoring it to a specific job. If you can get access to a word processor, then it is fairly easy to adapt your CV to the occasion. In any case, it is important to include a cover letter which briefly draws the employer's attention ('As you will see from my CV ...') to the information that will interest him most.

Passed by a second opinion: Writing about yourself isn't easy. The twin dangers of underselling yourself through modesty, or overselling yourself by trying too hard, overshadow each sentence. Most of us could use some help, especially if written communication isn't our number one talent. Look for someone who has successfully applied for jobs or get professional help from a careers centre.

What do I include?

Below is one example of a CV. It isn't a blueprint, as every CV should be unique to the person. There are other approaches, such as tailoring the CV to skills and achievements rather than job history, but in some form or other you should aim to cover the areas shown here.

CURRICULUM VITAE

JANET PARSONS

ADDRESS	21 Ashburn Drive, Potters Hill, Bath BA1 2UU
TELEPHONE	Work: 0454-54891 Home: 0225-63122
PERSONAL DETAILS	Date of Birth: 19th July 1969 Age: 21 years Nationality: British

EDUCATION

1980-87: GREENFIELD COMPREHENSIVE SCHOOL

GCSE 'O' Levels in:

Maths (C) English (B)
Physical Science (B)
Religious Education (C)
History (B)
Needlework (B)

GCSE 'A' Levels in:

English (C)
Religious Education (B)
History (C)

1987-90: LEICESTER POLYTECHNIC

BA Hons, 2:2 Combined Arts
(English, History, Politics)

WORK EXPERIENCE

1988 Summer job: Playscheme assistant (Bath City Council)

1989 Summer job: Tennis instructor (Redwood Camp, New York State, USA)

October 1990 to present: Assistant instructor (Hollytree Day Centre, supervising social and educational activities with adults with learning disabilities.)

OTHER EXPERIENCE	I have been involved in youth work with my local church – planning and leading a weekly programme of events for 12-16 year olds.
	Whilst at college, I wrote a regular review column in the college magazine. I was secretary of the tennis club and organized inter-college tournaments.
INTERESTS	I enjoy swimming, aerobics and theatre-going. I have my own car and am currently doing an evening course in vehicle maintenance.

alan macdonald

You, the job-hunter, are sitting in front of a potential employer perspiring and thinking how stressful the interview is for you. It may not occur to you that fear is behind almost

C H A P T E R

every interview question an employer asks. Any job-hunter will cope with the employer's questions if he or she keeps that in mind.

INTERVIEWS: WHAT EVERY EMPLOYER FEARS

No employer cares about your past. The only thing an employer cares about is your future. Therefore, the more a question *appears* to be about your past, the more certain you may be some fear lurks behind it. And that fear is about your future — what you will be like *after* the employer decides to take you on.

So let's run down typical employer interview questions — see what they are, then what the fear behind those questions is, and perhaps some key phrases that can be used in answering the questions – so as to allay the fear.

"... typical employer interview questions ..."

*t*ell me about yourself'

The fear behind the question: The employer is afraid they won't ask the right questions during the interview, and that there's something in your attitude that will make you a bad employee.

The point you try to get across to answer their fear: You would make a good employee, and you have proved this by your past.

Ideas or phrases you might use: A brief history of where you were brought up, hobbies, interests, *etc.*, as well as a brief description of where you have worked or the kind of work you have done. Also, any phrase describing your past attitude to your work in a positive way: 'hard worker', 'came in early, left late', *etc.*

*h*ave you ever done this kind of work before?'

The fear: The employer is afraid you can't do the work because you don't possess the necessary experience or skills.

Your answer: You have transferable skills.

Ideas or phrases: The same ones as in the last question. Plus: 'Every job is a new world but I make myself at home very quickly.'

*j*ust what kind of position are you looking for?'

The fear: That it isn't the same kind of job the employer needs to fill – *e.g.*, they are looking for a secretary, you are looking to be office manager;

they are looking for someone who can work alone, you are looking for a job where you would be rubbing shoulders with other people.

Your answer: You have picked up many skills which are transferable.

Ideas or phrases: You are looking for work where you can use your skills with people/data /things/machines/tools/plants/whatever (specify what skills you most enjoy).

If you are applying for a known vacancy, you can *first* respond to this question by saying, 'I'd be happy to answer that, but first it seems to me it's important for you to tell me what kind of work this post involves.' Once the employer has told you, couch your answer in terms of the skills you have which are relevant to the work the employer has described.

'Why did you leave your last job?' or 'How did you get along with your former boss and colleagues?'

The fear: The employer is afraid that you don't get along with people. Especially bosses.

Your answer: That you do get along well with people, and your attitude towards your former boss(es) and colleagues proves it.

Ideas or phrases: 'My boss and I both felt I would be happier and more effective in a job where ...' (here describe your strong points: *e.g.,* 'I would be under less supervision and have more room to use my creativity').

Say as many positive things as you can about your boss and colleagues.

*'h*ow much were you absent from work during your last job?'

The fear: The employer is afraid that you will be absent from work a lot.

Your answer: You Will Not Be Absent From Work.

Ideas or phrases: If you were absent quite a bit on a previous job, say why and stress that it is a past difficulty (if it is).

If you were not absent on your previous job, stress your good attendance record.

*'c*an you explain these gaps in your work history?'

The fear: The employer is afraid that you don't really like to work, and will resign the minute things aren't going 'your way'.

Your answer: You like to work and you regard times when things aren't going well as challenges.

Ideas or phrases: You were working hard during the times when you weren't employed: studying, doing volunteer work, trying to get beyond 'keeping busy' to finding a sense of mission for your life.

*'d*oesn't this work (or this job) represent a step down for you?'

The fear: The employer is afraid that you will leave as soon as you are offered a better job.

Your answer: You will stick with this job as long as you and the employer agree this is where you should be.

Ideas or phrases: 'Every employer is afraid the

''... finding a sense of mission in your life ...''

employee will leave too soon, and every employee is afraid the employer might fire him. I'll do a great job here, and I'll stay as long as we agree this is where I should be.'

*'t*ell me, what is your greatest weakness?'

The fear. The employer is afraid you have some work-flaw and is hopeful you will confess to it now.

Your answer: You have limitations just like any other person, but you work constantly to improve them.

Ideas or phrases: Mention some weakness of yours that has a positive aspect to it, *e.g.,* 'I don't respond well to being over supervised, because I have a great deal of initiative, and I like to use it.'

There are many other interview questions we could look at, but I think you get the idea. Given this understanding − that the employer is under as much stress in the job interview as you are − you can listen hard to an employer's interview questions, ask yourself what fears lie behind those questions, and know how to answer them.

richard nelson bolles

Taken from *What Color is Your Parachute?* © 1990 by Richard Nelson Bolles. Published by Ten Speed Press, Berkeley, CA. Used by permission of the publisher.

JOB INTERVIEW CHECKLIST

Have you ever come away from an interview knowing you haven't done yourself justice? Or found reasons not to apply for a job because you were secretly terrified of being grilled in the interview? Or is your problem actually getting as far as the interview stage in the first place?

1. Informational interviews. *It may never have occurred to you, but it is possible for job seekers to set up interviews as well as employers. Narrow down your field of interest to a specific area then ask yourself if you know anyone who may have contacts in that field. Telephone the company asking for the contact by name. When you are through to them say something on the lines of, 'My name is Jane Brown. I'd like to ask your professional advice. I'm interested in the field of retail management and I'd appreciate any direction you can give me in my job search.' You may be surprised to find how many interviews you get where you are asking the questions. These are not job interviews, but employers are impressed by initiative. You will gain information and experience and, if you leave a CV behind, maybe eventually a job as well.*

2. Do your homework. *Everyone gets flustered when they are asked an unexpected question or are unprepared for what an interview throws at them. The best way is to do your homework both on the company and what you wish to communicate in the interview. Find out what you can about the company. Read any publication or talk to anyone who knows them. A genuine and well informed compliment about some aspect of their product or service will be well received. Write out the points you want to get across about yourself beforehand and prepare some intelligent questions you can ask.*

3. Dreaded questions. *Most of us go into an interview knowing we have weak points and gaps in our experience. A good interviewer will spot these immediately and probe our weaknesses. Rather than being defensive it helps to have thought through your weaknesses and to have ready answers. Every weak point has a positive flipside that can be expressed to your advantage. For example, if you are inexperienced in something you can stress the fresh approach and energy you will bring to task.*

4. Nerves. *Interview nerves are familiar to nearly everyone. If the other applicants look cool and untroubled, this may just be the front they put up to deal with their nerves.*

One reassuring fact to remember is that interviewers are sometimes just as unsure and anxious as you are. They are worried about choosing the wrong person and have often not had any real training in interview techniques themselves. Therefore the more you can put them at ease, the more you will feel at east too. Don't fold your arms defensively – adopt a relaxed physical posture (without sprawling!) and resist temptation to jiggle your foot, drum your fingers, etc.

Having prayed that God's will be done over a job we must trust him. Remember when you're in the interview, the worst that could possibly happen is that they don't offer you the job – and that doesn't mean the end of your career.

alan macdonald

i remember *saying* once, with the certainty one has only as a final year student: 'Well, I'm sorry, but life doesn't get much more real than this.' I'm sure at the time I believed I was perfectly

justified in considering the travails, the long gruelling hours and intense pressures of writing essays to be just as demanding as anything

THE TRUTH ABOUT FIRST JOBS

the 'real world' could hurl at me. Now of course, I know better; now I have a job. And one thing your first real let's-get-this-career-started job teaches you is that what you know about the workings of your chosen field, and indeed of life in general, could fit on the ballpoint of the sterling silver Parker pen your parents gave you for graduation.

Many of my friends have chosen to adhere to the age-old philosophy 'When the going gets

"Now of course, I know better ..."

tough, the tough go on postgraduate courses.' But they are only stalling the inevitable (I mean, there are only so many PhDs available), and soon they will face the grim realities of the working world.

r eal life

So for those of my friends still dawdling in the halls of higher education, here are a few of the traumas you can expect.

1. No syllabus. Remember the reassuring feel of that freshly photocopied hand-out, how precise and complete it was? It gave you a sense of order and security — whenever all those about you seemed to be losing their heads and yours felt none too steady, you reached for your trusty syllabus ('Ah, March 23 — Plato's Theory of Forms; no wonder I'm confused!'). Most important, was a promise of completion; no matter how gruesome the subject, it too would pass.

No such luck in the real world. Oh, yes, there are deadlines and schedules, but they have none of the sweet finite nature of the syllabus. You find yourself trapped in a life of agenda promiscuity — you finish one, toss it away, and there's another staring into your early-morning face. And these agendas can't be trusted. The unexpected happens, priorities change: an emergency meeting, a gained or lost account, a writer with cold feet, and suddenly you're adrift with nothing to go on but hastily dashed-off notes and cryptic mutterings from your boss as she (wisely) heads out the door. You have only your wits and adrenaline (put your money on the adrenaline) with which to decide how fast is 'soon' and where is this supposed to go after I'm

"You have only your wits and adrenaline ..."

finished with it anyway? Here's where close contact with the cleaning staff is vital. They've seen 'em come and they've seen 'em go – they know who does what and how well ... in fact, talkative cleaning people are even more reliable than the syllabus and they don't get lost a week before finals.

2. Reserved seats. As the lowest person on the totem pole, you get the seat everybody started with (and fought like mad to get out of, and that's part of the reason everyone is so nice to you on the first day). Easily recognizable by its lack of window and privacy, it will be a veritable home from home. Get used to it; you'll be sitting there for eight hours each day. Suddenly the lyrics of jailhouse ballads make perfect sense. Don't fight it; breathe into it, make these walls your own. For your own sanity and circulation, make friends in other departments and wander occasionally. Don't worry, your boss will understand; temporary paralysis is not a pretty sight.

"... week-long parties and sleeping late ..."

3. Holidays. Cast your mind back to the days of championship tans, day-trips, week-long parties and sleeping late for an entire month because you 'deserved it'. Hope you took pictures because in the real world the word 'break' is preceded by coffee, not Easter, Christmas or summer.

But the body is an amazing thing – at any given time during the last week of June, you may find yourself suddenly and inexplicably at the station with nothing in your hand but sunglasses and your student card. This will pass with time.

4. Skiving off. These two words cease to have any meaning whatsoever in your life. Don't even think about them. Here, the absence of a window

"... treasure these moments."

from the vicinity of the new employee's desk is explained. This allows you the illusion that it's always raining and you're better off inside anyway. Even if the sunshine from someone else's window beckons you, no, you cannot skip out after lunch with the rationalization that your friends will take notes for you. In the real world, a pleasure trip is when you are allowed across the street to the sandwich-bar for coffee. And you'll learn to treasure these moments.

5. Weekends. The word Friday, however, takes on new and meaningful dimensions for the recently hired employee. For the first couple of weeks, you can expect to wander through Saturday and Sunday with a doomed conviction that there's something incredibly important you really should be doing. Surely there's an essay to write, a seminar to prepare, a dozen chapters to read somewhere. Guilt mounts as you catch yourself leisurely reading novels, strolling through the park, watching (gasp) TV. Relax. Enjoy; it's the best reason there is for staying out of postgraduate studies.

6. Packed lunches. If your mother, smitten with the frantic nostalgia found most often in the parent of the recent graduate, saved your old Snoopy or Paddington Bear lunch box, get it back. You can afford neither the cost nor the time of eating lunch out. What, do you want your boss to think you really don't need that rise?

"You are fired ..."

7. Politeness. Gone are the days when you could look your professor squarely in the eye and say, 'Yeah, well, I think Sartre was full of wind.' Tell your boss you think what she's just said is full of wind and she will not say, 'Now, that's an

interesting observation; why do you think so?'
No. She will say 'You are fired', if she says
anything at all. This isn't to say swallow your
opinions and all your fresh and maybe even
innovative ideas and nod like those horrible toy
dogs in the rear windows of battered Capris, but
for your own sake (as well as your Mother's —
heaven knows she tried), be polite. Firm but
polite. Usually you will receive the same
consideration, but even if you don't, you may
comfort yourself with the fact that you are the
better person — the better and still employed
person.

8. Exam grades. The good news is that you don't
have to sweat for them anymore. No longer is
your entire future based on three multiple choice
tests with 40% of the correct answers being 'D:
None of the above' just to confuse you. But gone
also is the ability to measure your progress in
yearly intervals. Just because you hand all your
assignments in on time and no-one seems to wish
you'd never darkened this establishment's door,
it does not mean you will be promoted to editor-
in-chief at the end of May. In real life, you cannot
pass exams for anything.

r eal people

Now, I don't mean to paint too gloomy a picture.
There are a few shining points in the world of the
first-time employee. You do get a cheque every
month, and during the 45 minutes you wait in
line at the bank, you can gaze at it lovingly and
pretend you will actually see some of it. And
remember when you, sitting so straight in your
sincere interviewing suit, smiled winningly at
your employer-to-be and said, 'I want to work in

*"... gosh, I
just like
people ..."*

"I like some people ..."

this field because I believe communication skills are my strong point and, gosh, I just like people'? Well, here they are, those said people, simply clamouring for your attention. Whether it's to let you know they never heard of you and 'whatever happened to that "nice girl" who used to answer the phones?' or to remind you that the London office needs those ('Oh, did I say seventeen? I meant seventy') contract copies yesterday, or just to interrupt the long-distance phone call your story depends on to inquire where you want these boxes and 'Could you sign this here, here, and here?' – these wonderful people want to make you an integral part of their lives. When next you interview for a job, be more prudent; don't make rash statements. 'I like some people' will get you in enough trouble.

I often wonder (and wonder aloud to the annoyance of my friends) why those safely ensconced in academe take it upon themselves to remain so uncharacteristically mute about the real world. Are they simply trying to lessen the competition in the academic world by encouraging undergraduates to 'get a real job', or did they have an actual psychological block? Why was I learning about photosynthesis, which will take place throughout eternity unaffected by my knowledge or ignorance, when I should have been learning how to convince the electricity board that the lights in the entire office really did go off?

mary mcnamara

First published as 'Assigned seat, required attendance and weekends off: the truth about first jobs' by Mary McNamara, MS Magazine, October 1986.

IS IT HARDER FOR WOMEN?

'My boss in my first job made my life an absolute misery. I desperately tried to please him, I had lots of ideas, but I kept asking "what is it I'm doing wrong?" Looking back I think he was threatened by my personality and enthusiasm – because I am a woman.'
                                                              Jill

10

In our equality conscious age, sexual discrimination has become an issue where once it was a fact of working life. It is quite possible that as a young woman entering the career world, you will meet with the same respect and opportunities as a man. Sadly that may not always be the case. Like Jill, women may meet hostile or patronizing attitudes from some men. The best way of retaining confidence in your own abilities is to recognize prejudice for what it is. Here are three typical situations that you may come up against:

1. The male club. There are still some professions which are largely male dominated. Being the only woman can be undermining and leave you feeling isolated. 'In the first meeting I have to go in strong. If I let them "little girl" me in the first five minutes I'm lost', says one female architect about site meetings. It is important to think through how you'll cope with being in a minority if it's inevitable in your profession. If you're single, sharing accommodation with another female may prove a healthy safety valve.

2. Flirts and snubs. There are two main ways men can use to put women down. One is to flirt and never take you seriously, the other is to freeze you out by ignoring your contribution. Either reaction is a sign that a man feels threatened by you in some way. Confrontation may not be the best way of dealing with this as the man may not even be aware of what he is doing. Perhaps the best approach is to keep your cool

'' ... a healthy safety valve.''

"... women at work are more vulnerable ..."

and be determined that you won't let yourself be intimidated. In time your male colleague may learn to respect your views and realize that you aren't out to threaten his status.

3. Self-doubt. Everyone suffers from this at some point, but it has been said that women at work are more vulnerable than most. Jill believes a woman has to be more confident about her abilities than a man, as she'll often be surrounded by male role-models. Somewhere deep inside a voice keeps whispering, 'They'll find you out eventually, you'll never be as good.' Society's continuing emphasis on women's true vocation being in childbirth and home-making can add to the feeling of being an 'imposter' at work.

The working world can be hard at times. For every Christian what counts is to have your security rooted in the unchangeable – Jesus' love for you. Whilst on earth Jesus was a man who accepted women as unique and important. Despite the patriarchal Jewish society, Jesus spent time talking to women and valuing their company. Women play major roles in the gospel story, they are certainly not inferior or shadowy figures cooking the meals in the background.

"... the battle of the sexes ..."

Whatever the working world communicates to a woman, she has the same right to be there as a man. In fact most workplaces would suffer noticeably if women were absent. God has created us male and female to be complementary. As Christians we shouldn't be drawn into 'the battle of the sexes', but work towards a positive acceptance of our different strengths.

*t*he dread-ed ques-tion. It can come in many shapes and forms. Some-times it comes disguised as an innocent en-quiry about what you're doing this weekend. Sometimes it is

C H A P T E R

thrown at you out of the blue: 'Why don't you swear?' 'What book are you reading?' or 'I think all relig-ions are the same, don't you?'

WITNESS AT WORK

Here is the opportunity. The one you prayed for. The chance to throw in a meaningful comment that might eventually lead to your friend's conversion.

But no meaningful comments come to mind. Instead you feel yourself go hot. Your tongue sticks to the roof of your mouth and you are conscious that you are spilling coffee down your trousers. You finally make a strange gargling noise and bring out, 'Oh, um..., I don't know ...'

by which time the moment has gone and the conversation moved on to why the government doesn't do something about x, y or z.

*S*tarting out

Taking on our first job can be a crisis time for personal evangelism. The pressures upon us to succeed are great. We have never done the job before. Will we be able to cope? How will we get on with the people at work? Will they accept us or put us through some initiation test like offering us the boss's mug to drink from? All our instincts are to conform. To make ourselves as much like everyone else as possible. Ideally to pass ourselves off as someone who has worked there for years.

There is a problem with this chameleon instinct. Our faith doesn't merge in too well with the background. Christ never offered conformity as an option to his followers. He calls us to be different. To stand against the tide of compromise, indifference, selfishness and malice in our work place. The assurance that Christians will be liked by everyone is notably absent from the New Testament. Faith will sometimes even meet with opposition. It was Christ's very outspokenness that offended the Pharisees.

Is our work place the right situation to think about sharing our faith though? If we are employed by someone to do a job, shouldn't we leave all thoughts of evangelism outside the front door when we arrive? Plausible as this sounds, there are good reasons to believe God calls us to witness at work.

The first is simple. Jesus told us to. No, he didn't say 'become an accountant because there are great opportunities for evangelism in

"Jesus told us to."

accountancy'. Jesus doesn't talk about specific situations that we should exploit. He says, 'Go into *all the world* and preach the Good News.' There is an assumption behind that which says that there is no place we can cross off our list. This doesn't mean we are expected to be non-stop evangelists, handing out tracts as we board the bus. It does mean that we need to be prepared 'to give an account of our faith' to any one person at any time. This includes the manager at work or the cleaning lady who empties the bins. As far as God is concerned there is no distinction. That's worth remembering when you're next summoned to head office!

(Mark 16:15)

You're stuck with them

When you start a job you may be thrown into a closed environment where you have little choice who you mix with. The people may be very different in age from you and it's almost certain they'll have different temperaments and tastes from yours. You may even find none of your work colleagues would be people you'd naturally choose to spend your leisure time with. The fact remains you will see more of them than most people. Up to forty hours a week — that's more than some married couples see of each other!

Given this amount of time in their company, you will get to know them on a long term basis. The way they talk, their moods, possibly the irritating way they grind their teeth when they're thinking. Before you write them off, remember they will get to know you too. They will notice how you react under pressure. They will see the real you. It has often been remarked that the quality of our lives is the best advert for our Christian faith. The people we work alongside

''... they will get to know you too ...''

get a better chance than most to watch the
adverts.

Some time ago the church I belonged to
decided it was time to do some door to door
evangelism. I was among the many who in-
wardly winced at the prospect of knocking on
someone's door and trying to witness to a total
stranger.

The reality in fact surprised me. Quite a few
people shut the door quickly, but quite a few
were prepared to stop and chat. As I grew in
boldness and tried out new ways of opening up
a conversation I began to think I had quite a gift
as an evangelist. By the time we left the last house
I was convinced I was the next Billy Graham. Yet
on reflection afterwards I realized why, for me,
it had been easy. There was no involvement.
These strangers were people I would probably
never meet again. I could say what I liked. Not
so the people I worked with. There was more at
stake in seeing them every day, but more reality
to my witness too. It wasn't just a case of winning
a conversation but of being Christ's flesh and
blood representative amongst people who gave
him no place.

*"The reality
in fact sur-
prised me ..."*

Who do you admire?

If we think about the people we really look up to
it is rarely because they are good talkers. It is the
fabric of their lives that impresses us, the way
they deal with success and failure. It helps to
remember that the people you are going to work
alongside are probably no different. In the long
run, whether you are good at winning arguments
or sprinkling conversations with Scriptural
quotations is not likely to make much difference.
They will never guess you are a Christian unless

you tell them, but they will never know what a Christian is unless you *show* them.

It is easy to focus on negative qualities here. Christians are often marked out in their work place because they don't swear, don't get drunk or because they keep out of the sweepstakes. But it is the positive qualities that really stand out. At work we are often under pressure. Each person has their own responsibilities and is anxious not to get the rap for anything that goes wrong. The result is often that people have little time for each other. An act of kindness like remembering a workmate's birthday, making them a drink or just listening to their problems can be an oasis in a harsh world. People will notice such things.

*W*ised up

There are limits to be defined here. It wouldn't be difficult to become the resident 'agony aunt' at work and never find time for the job. Even worse, Christians can appear to be a soft touch. There will always be those who will exploit a willingness to help. Jesus said we are to be 'wise as serpents and innocent as doves'. The wise part is knowing how and when to say 'no'. It's important to learn how to do this without offending others. Cultivate being firm and friendly rather than curt and embarrassed. Explain your reasons and in most cases people will understand. They are under the same pressure as you.

All of this concentrates on how to 'be' in your workplace rather than what to say. This is quite intentional. 'But what do I say to them?' you may ask. 'How do I get round to talking about my faith?'

There are whole books written about this

"People will notice such things ..."

Paul E. Little
How to Give Away Your Faith, (IVP, 2nd edition 1989)

*"Time will be
in short
supply ..."*

Rebecca Manley Pippert,
Out of the Salt Shaker
(IVP, 1979)

which go into details that this chapter cannot. What is worth saying here is to forget some of the things you did at school or college. Long rambling conversations that started with arguing about Tracey Chapman's lyrics over coffee and concluded with life, God and the universe at 2.00 a.m. are not the stuff of a working life. Time will be in short supply. Conversations may be cut short by a phone call or the end of coffee break.

Evangelism is much more about sprinkling a pinch of salt here and there than getting into meaty discussions. And when the end of the day comes? Then perhaps the real opportunities arise in our leisure time. If you've shown you are someone who listens, if you can be a good friend, if you've earned their respect. After all, evangelism isn't something 'you shouldn't do to your dog, let alone a friend'. Evangelism is about people.

TIGHT CORNERS YOU MAY FACE

*1. **Language** at work may be more colourful than the clothes of the loudest dresser. We may well work alongside someone who uses swear words like commas in a sentence. When blasphemy is part of the common vocabulary, it can be hard on the ears and presents us with the dilemma of whether we ought to object. James 3:10 is clear about our personal responsibility: 'Out of the same mouth come praising and cursing ... this should not be.' However hard it may seem Christians cannot join in with the swearing to be thought 'one of the boys/girls'. But should we take issue with others' language? 'If anyone is never at fault in what he says, he is a perfect man ...' adds James. In other words, everyone has problems with controlling the tongue. It isn't our job to judge others'*

speech, it is God's. This said, there may come a time when a person's continued use of the Lord's name as a swear word becomes intolerably offensive. If so, try taking them on one side and explaining why — it has probably never occurred to them what they are saying.

2. Dishonesty may be a problem in the same way. Small acts of dishonesty like overclaiming expenses or fiddling time sheets are often taken for granted. 'Everybody does it' and you may find the pressure to conform is very real. Setting a standard of honesty for yourself is easiest if you take a stand the first time. Excusing our conscience once makes it easier to do next time. Remember that what we do is our responsibility, what others do is theirs. There is no need to broadcast our honesty to make others feel guilty. The hardest situation is one where a workmate wants to involve you in something that isn't strictly honest. Saying 'no' will never be popular, but we have to seriously ask ourselves if saying 'no' to God is the other option.

3. Religion-bashing can often be a popular item on the menu when any group of people get together over coffee or lunch. Some news item about Ireland or the Middle East can be the cue for someone to start in on how all religious people are hypocrites, brainless or fanatical murderers. The conversations are rarely serious discussions and entering into 'a religious argument' is unlikely to have any good effect. The choices are to keep quiet, leave or turn the discussion into something more positive. If the third can be achieved it is worth doing. Saying, 'Well, I'm a Christian and ...' may shock your listeners into taking the subject seriously. You may find your view isn't without support. However, fruitless argument and 'Christian-baiting' are times to use discretion. Save your words for a better occasion.

alan macdonald

money talks, but what does it say? In the form of a crisp, new, first ever pay-cheque it says, 'You've arrived. Treat yourself. You deserve it. What about that cassette

and CD player you've always promised yourself?'

Later it winks at you in green numbers on the auto-bank screen: '£52.60 DR.'

THE TWO-FACED PAY-CHEQUE

'Overdrawn,' it says, 'I warned you. One pay-cheque and you think you're Richard Branson.'

talking money

Money talks. And we all listen whether we admit it or not. We Christians are not materialistic of course, we just want a good job, a comfortable house, a reasonable car, one decent holiday a year (the Greek islands would do) ... no more than anybody else – but no less either. Is that materialism?

Twenty years ago, broadly speaking, the poorer a Christian was, the more spiritual he or she was considered. Today the pendulum has swung the other way. Spirituality goes hand in hand with prosperity. Part of this is to do with the spirit of our age. We live in the enterprise society. Where community spirit or patriotism were the watchwords for previous generations, 'wealth creation' is what we honour today.

Profit is the great god of our society. All activities stand or fall by it. Close behind comes the need to consume. 'I buy therefore I am' as someone has put it. New inducements to shop spill through our letter box every day: better terms, lower interest, unbeatable offers. Yesterday it was essential to have a video, today I can't do without a personal computer.

"I buy there-fore I am ..."

Christians are often unknowingly influenced by society's trends. But the idea that God's blessing equals personal prosperity is one which many would argue from the Bible. It is there in black and white, they say, in verses such as 'Delight yourself in the Lord and he will give you the desires of your heart' and 'God richly provides us with everything for our enjoyment.' And in Paul's numerous references to the 'riches' of our glorious inheritance.

(Psalm 31)

(1 Timothy 6:17)

From passages like this, we're assured, we can see that God wants his children to have the very best in life. We're advised to settle for nothing less. Our God owns the treasure houses of the universe; would he be miserly with the salary you need to live comfortably? No, he wants you to live like the son of a king. He wants you to lay hold on his promises, 'to name it and claim it' if you want it in slogan terms.

*P*rosperity gospel

This sort of 'prosperity gospel' teaching originates in America and many popular preachers and churches subscribe to it. One way of attracting the unconverted is by painting pictures of rich, healthy Christians thriving under God's blessing. The influence of this sort of thinking in Britain is more subtle but nonetheless real. Middle class goals and affluent values can be passed off as Christian.

It isn't difficult to see why 'prosperity thinking' is attractive. Everyone would like to be rich and healthy! The idea that God rewards our service and holy living with material benefits appeals to our sense of fair play. We dedicate our lives to God and he looks after our interests. Rather like having a good agent.

There are several half-truths in all of this, but the sum total is a distortion of God's character. That he wants the best for his children is true ... but money and a houseful of consumer goods may not be the best. He wants to grant 'the desires of our heart', but the context of the Psalm is firmly on delight in God and not in mammon. Similarly we are heirs to great riches but Paul quite clearly has in mind 'the riches of God's grace' rather than healthy bank accounts. Prosperity teaching also ignores Jesus' stress on the cost of following him rather than the material benefits (see *Mark 10:17-21* and chapter 14 'What if I don't land the perfect job?').

To talk in terms of 'naming and claiming' things is to reduce God to the level of a chocolate machine, where all we need to do is push the right button. In reality God is a person who cares for us far more than to pander to our every whim.

''... reduce God to the level of a chocolate machine ...''

(Ephesians 2:7)

*b*ad money

How does this apply to our first pay-cheque then? Should we seal up the envelope neatly and return it to our employer with a polite note saying, 'No thanks, I'm a Christian'? Or throw it in the nearest litter bin along with the Coke cans and apple cores? If money is the root of all evil, surely we're better off not touching it at all?

In fact somebody taking this view (I've never met them) would be misquoting the Bible at the other extreme. It is not money, but the love of money that is called the root of all kinds of evil. The pay-cheque in your pocket is a neutral piece of paper. To put it another way, money is two-faced, it can be an instrument of either good or evil. It is why you want it and how you use it that counts.

(1 Timothy 6:10)

It's strange that something we're all eager to have should lead to all kinds of evil. Perhaps it is that very eagerness which can have the disastrous effects. People who talk constantly about money, their lack of it, their need for it and how to get it, can be more materialistic than the richest millionaire. There is no virtue in poverty itself. Often it is what we lack that makes us eager to point the finger at someone better off. Feeling pious in our poverty we are blind to the envy that has crept into our thinking.

"Anxiety over money ..."

Anxiety over money is another common disease. It's all too easy for a desire to live within our means to spill over into Scrooge-like tendencies. If you're always too slow off the mark to buy the coffee, miserliness is beginning to get a hold. Again, it's easy to justify our behaviour as thriftiness – something we're taught as a childhood virtue. But this is more a middle class value than a New Testament one.

When the Bible does talk about money it's a notable (and uncomfortable) fact that it's often in terms of giving it away. How much we should earn is never answered. That we should be willing to share whatever we have is left in no doubt.

(Mark 10:21; 2 Corinthians 8:7)

*t*he eye of the needle

Jesus doesn't say it is impossible to be a rich Christian, but he does say how difficult it is for the rich to enter the kingdom. Camels squeezing through needle eyes is the size of the problem. Paul develops this. The rich are in danger of putting their hope in their riches rather than in God. They should 'do good, be rich in good deeds and willing to share'.

(Mark 10:28)

(1 Timothy 6:18)

That's the rich then, but 'thank goodness you and I aren't numbered among the rich!' we say. Have you ever noticed that nobody admits to being wealthy these days? Film stars and best-selling authors deny the very possibility in chat shows. It makes us feel better if the rich person is always someone else.

"... a damp archway near London's Waterloo station ..."

But of course, this cuts both ways. I recently saw rows of cardboard boxes under a damp archway near London's Waterloo station. People of all ages were living and sleeping in them. By their standards we are the rich. An Ethiopian child sitting down to dinner with us would be goggle-eyed at the luxury in our house and on our plates.

When Paul talks about sharing our wealth, it's clear he's thinking of every Christian, not just the wealthy (whoever they are). *'Each man should give what he has decided in his heart to give, not reluctantly or under compulsion, for God loves a cheerful giver.'*

(2 Corinthians 9:7)

In this sentence the word 'cheerful' is as hard as the word 'give'. Money for Christians can become a list of do's and don'ts, reminders and rebukes. When someone stands up at the front of church and says they're going to talk about giving, how do you feel? Cheerful? 'Guilty' is a better word in my case!

Subconsciously we may even think that God wants us to feel guilty about money. But God is never the author of false guilt. It's one of the devil's favourite weapons with Christians. Paul's advice means we ought to be able to look at our pay-cheque with a clear and glad conscience. Decide and give cheerfully – not reluctantly, not under compulsion. Then enjoy what God gives to you. If we go out for a meal and can't enjoy it because 'the money could have been better spent' then we are simply not appreciating God's goodness to us in our freedom. What a terrible shame if Christians are known as the most self-sacrificial, but also the most joyless of people.

"What a terrible shame ..."

THE FANTASTIC PLASTIC TRAP

Any chapter on money would be incomplete without some reference to the modern 'answer' to financial problems: credit.

'Annual income twenty pounds, annual expenditure nineteen, nineteen and six, result happiness. Annual income twenty pounds, annual expenditure twenty pounds nought and six, result misery!' So says Mr Micawber in Dickens' David Copperfield. Today Mr Micawber would no doubt be offered a Master card, American Express or a personal account at any high street store. On top of that he could take advantage of bank loans, finance companies, a second mortgage

and 'attractive interest terms' on everything he ha[s] ever wanted.

'Neither a borrower or lender be' wrot[e] Shakespeare. But he never faced the credit explosio[n] of our age. And surely most people will have to borro[w] at some point, for example to buy a house or a ca[r] necessary for work?

Christian Arena,
September 1988.

The Bible doesn't say that all borrowing is wrong[.] In fact as Paul Mills says 'Lending was a vital part o[f] the welfare system of ancient Israel.' Two proviso[s] have to be added to this however. Firstly, borrowin[g] was seen as a last resort for the poor rather than as [a] way of life for everyone. Secondly, taking interest wa[s] clearly forbidden and outstanding debts wer[e] cancelled after seven years. In other words lending wa[s] seen simply as a means of poor relief.

(Exodus 22:25)

Nevertheless the importance of repaying your debt[s] is clearly stressed in both the Old and New Testaments[.] In fact our only outstanding debt should be to love on[e] another.

(Romans 13:8)

Today using credit cards can be just a convenien[t] way of deferring payment until the end of the month[.] It is difficult to see how this, in itself, is going agains[t] Christian principles. The dangers are hidden though[,] like rocks under the surface of a calm sea.

"The dangers are hidden though ..."

Although using credit cards doesn't have to mea[n] paying interest, 60% of people in Britain will do so. It'[s] easy to see why. Credit cards can deceive us int[o] treating them as plastic rather than hard cash. It feel[s] like we're getting something for nothing. In the sam[e] way, shops offer us 'instant credit' with no down-payment. We walk out of the shop with a video, having paid nothing. Of course payment comes tomorrow and sometimes for years afterwards, but it's all too easy to put that out of our minds.

On top of this the interest we pay on credit cards is high (currently around 23%). The result is that often our debts mount up rather than being paid off. We are caught up in financial slavery; the first claim on our money is the lender's rather than God's. Many people, often in the under thirties age bracket, have fallen into the debt pit where it seems impossible ever to climb out. Christians might pray to God, 'the eternal banker', to bail them out, but he will not always shield us from the consequences of our own actions.

What should Christians do about credit then? Perhaps the best use of credit cards is to take a pair of scissors and cut them into tiny pieces. Certainly if debt has become a problem for you, I would recommend it.

"... cut them into tiny pieces ..."

Not so friendly

If we admit there may be times when we are forced to borrow, there are some precautions we can at least take:

1. Count the cost beforehand and don't gamble on being able to meet the repayments later.

2. Refuse to pay high interest rates. Bank loans are better than credit cards and borrowing from friends or parents may sometimes be a better alternative still.

3. If you do use credit cards, treat them like cash. Write down the amounts spent so you're aware of what's left in the bank.

4. Before borrowing on anything ask yourself if it's part of God's will or just our consumer-mad society.

The two-faced pay-cheque needs wise hand-ling. Those early days in a job are likely to set a pattern for the rest of your life. The greatest lie of our society is to say that money and its power should dictate our priorities. Jesus had a simple answer to this – choose. You can't serve God and mammon.

Want to know more?

To learn more about money matters (and the important subject of tithing) you can read Pennies for Heaven by Ian Coffey (Kingsway, 1984).

alan macdonald

*t*he minis-ter looked out at the congregation. Towards the back sat Mark, fresh from college with a newly-minted degree. He would begin his first 'real' job on Monday. This was his

first time in a small-town church.

The minister cleared his throat. 'I hope you all done your Scripture reading.' Mark winced.

HOW TO SURVIVE YOUR LOCAL CHURCH

Not a grammar snob, Mark nevertheless felt shaken by the end of the service. He was not alone, other new graduates were floundering in similar situations. In local churches where the minister is not John Stott. In churches where the biblical teaching rivalled only the hymns in shallowness. They found themselves squirming in their pews.

'Christian Unions train leaders for the local

church!' a friend once proclaimed enthusi-
astically. His words haunted me later in a fog-
bound part of the Norfolk coast as I trudged past
potholes to the church. My local congregation,
like Mark's, did not thrill me.

Getting that first degree had brought a certain
naive wonder and delight. For a while I felt
perfectly sure that 'All Things Bright and
Beautiful' meant me. It was a let-down to
discover that the world did not share this awe.
I felt brainy and bright, but terribly isolated in
every sense; my phone bills proved that. We
college and school-leavers could talk to each
other long distance more easily than we could
talk to our neighbours.

"... my phone bills proved that ..."

f itting in

Growing up is never easy. Adjusting to the adult
nonacademic world comes as a jolt to many. The
local church can present real problems — as we
confront old age face to face and try to relate to
it, or encounter total ignorance of areas we've
been taught are crucial.

*But why go to a prayer meeting with all the old
ladies?* many ask. The obvious answer is that we
go to prayer meetings to pray, not to flirt. The
absence of young people shouldn't matter. It
does, of course. But that's more my problem than
the church's. It is very easy to let other people
keep us from going to church. But it's a mistake.

Once during a church service I glanced around
me in dismay. Conventional middle-aged
couples! Elderly women! The few young ones all
had braces on their teeth. What a dull group to
be with!

But what a great group to die with! flashed
through my mind. Suppose terrorists burst into

the room and took us hostage? That curly permed woman on the piano bench would probably come through bravely. Others would do acts of great self-sacrifice. As ludicrous as the scene may sound, I saw each member in a new light. Everyone in that congregation was a person of value.

Criticism of the saints is an idle peace-time activity. In the urgency of war we don't have time for that. We draw together and get on with the job. We don't care about who is standing next to us – as long as he or she is competent.

Do we think we're living in peace today? All around us the spiritual battle is raging. If we toddle into a prayer meeting and find six old ladies, then we should rejoice. Elderly believers are the backbone of the church. They are the seasoned old veterans when it comes to prayer. We should be as glad to see them as Saul's troops were glad to see David. Goliath-like forces of spiritual wickedness lurk on all sides.

"... the backbone of the church ..."

the Peter Pan syndrome

The sermon was a dead loss and the rambling pastoral prayer clocked in at fourteen and a half minutes (an actual record noted by the author). Clearly this was not the diet usually served up at Christian Union meetings. Yet this is the only evangelical church in the area. What is the newcomer to do?

He or she faces three alternatives: give in to discontent, run away or adjust. Most people who have taken abuse for Jesus' sake amongst their friends do not set out to disrupt the local church upon arrival. Being a malcontent holds no appeal. Yet the eager young adult almost feels overqualified for the role of church member.

Many people get stuck here. They look hard at the unappealing new environment around them and rosily recall the good old days at the Christian Union. They yearn for the vibrant fellowship. They can taste the excitement of arriving at a houseparty and meeting old friends. They miss the stimulation. So ... almost without thinking, they look for ways of staying in education. Like Peter Pan, they opt for childhood. Here it's safe.

Adulthood, like yogurt, is an acquired taste. If the newcomer wishes to adjust to the new world without a syllabus then there is help. Much of the battle is spiritual.

*S*nob appeal

It helps to know the Lord's standard. Are you ill at ease at after-church coffee, but right at home in a physics lab? Then consider these words from Romans: *'Let us have no imitation Christian love ... Don't become snobbish but take a real interest in ordinary people. Don't become set in your own opinions.'*

How can I take a real interest in someone who turns me off? She wears brown dungarees and a pony-tail. When she left school at sixteen everybody was glad. What shall we talk about? Nail polish?

Or what about him? Fifty years old and thinks a good church social consists of food. Half the time he doesn't even wait for grace to be said. What do we talk about? Tuna casserole?

But we are told not to be snobbish. We dare not despise persons God loves. In his eyes there are no ordinary people. Each one is special. Each one was known by the Creator before the beginning of time. If they seem uninteresting to us, then we need to have our eyes checked.

"Much of the battle is spiritual ..."

(Romans 12:9, 16, Phillips)

"What do we talk about? Tuna casserole?"

'I see men as trees walking!' exclaimed a partially cured blind man. Jesus restored his vision completely. He can restore our eyes so that we can see people clearly. Not as trees walking, but as persons in their own right.

We don't have that kind of love in ourselves. When tempted to be snobbish, ask him to love through you. We need his love and we must follow his example. Jesus left his place with the Father and 'stripped himself of all privilege by consenting to be a slave by nature'. He came down to our level, humbling himself even to die a criminal's death.

(Philippians 2:7, Phillips)

Somehow that brings any exasperation with fellow believers into perspective. Humility is a new subject for most of us. I'll bet it wasn't your main subject at school. But it must be our goal.

*a*ge-barrier breakthrough

"Had age ever really been a barrier?"

Picture Mark, the mellowed newcomer soberly fitting into that same tiny church. As his mouth remains shut, he acquires wisdom. Through the long winter, he prays for sick people, for a bereaved family, for a man who has lost his job. He is invited to a wedding. One Wednesday night he asks for prayer himself. The people who seemed dull and ignorant at the beginning now have become precious to him. Could he ever have accused that congregation of ignorance? Had age ever really been a barrier?

Then he learns that age and ignorance were indeed barriers, but the other way round! 'When we first met you, you seemed so young!' he is told. 'You didn't seem to understand life.'

He can even grin. All along, that local minister had been praying for the ability to love him.

diane dadian

First published as 'How to survive in your local church' by Diane Dadian, *HIS Magazine*, June 1983.

ON YOUR OWN IN A NEW TOWN

'Here I am in my own flat, with my own job in a new town. Everything I'd always aimed for and it feels awful.'

Starting work away from home will be a shock to the system for many young adults fresh from school or college. It is hard to be prepared. Life has been geared to passing the exams and getting a job. Everything after that is the unknown — a vast adventure filled with exciting possibilities. The trouble is that when you first arrive the possibilities seem hard to find.

At school or college so much is on tap. There is the routine of study, lessons or lectures. There are your contemporaries, a whole crowd of similar age, outlook, tastes and sense of humour. There are the opportunities to forge friendships in the Christian Union, in sport, in long evenings just spent talking about nothing and everything.

A new job can produce a vacuum of relationships. As if everyone has suddenly left the room. It is as well to give some thought in advance to the changes that will be involved. If being a student offers an instant coffee existence, going out to work is more like brewing a pot of tea slowly. Friendships are not made overnight and your social calendar is unlikely to fill up the first week you hit town.

Where to start

Often the problem is where to start in making new relationships. At school or college they seem to happen just because you have a lot in common with your contemporaries. In a new town, with a new job, you will be unusually fortunate if the same thing happens. It's much more likely that you will need to take some initiatives.

"It is hard to be prepared."

"Work may not at first seem promising ..."

The Work Bench. *The obvious three areas to look for friends are at work, church and in leisure activities. Work may not seem promising at first. Quite possibly there will be few people in your immediate age group. It is natural to try and get to know the ones who are, but don't write off all other colleagues. One of the great experiences of a job is mixing with people of all different ages. Firm friendships can sometimes be formed with someone thirty years your senior.*

In the first weeks and months it is natural to be eager to make friends. I have often been aware of a 'trial period' in starting a job where work-mates are sizing you up. Trying to invite people for an evening out before they've got to know you a bit can be thought over-familiar. Once the 'new' tag has worn off a little, it may be possible to investigate after-work social events. If none seem to be happening try to start with individuals by inviting them out to a meal, a drink, a concert or other event. Be careful, though, that your social contacts are not restricted entirely to work.

The Pew. *Church is the next obvious field for social contact. Again (as the last chapter describes) your glance around the faces that fill the Sunday pews may not fill you with wild anticipation. But these people will be an invaluable support to you through the early days of loneliness and insecurity. Unlike the workplace there shouldn't be pressure to pretend that you're coping fine and are completely self-sufficient. If nobody attempts to draw you in, it may be worth approaching the minister or another leader and saying 'I'm new here, would you mind introducing me to a few people?' Suddenly a Sunday lunch invitation from the Smith family with the screaming baby takes on a new attractive light.*

Finding Christians of your own age that you can pray and talk with will not always be easy, but is certainly one of the things to look for in a church.

"I'm new here, ..."

The Leisure Centre. Lastly, moving away is a new start. There may be new ways of meeting friends that you haven't considered. Try drawing up a list of the interests, sports and hobbies you enjoy. Then draw up a second list of all the ones you've ever considered but have never got round to. Then start to hunt in the local newspaper, phone book and leisure centres for clubs that you could join. Sharing an activity with someone is still the best way to get to know them. I once spent ten weeks doing pottery classes when I was trying to establish myself in a new town. The result was one ugly slab pot but I enjoyed meeting some new people!

There are three things needed to enjoy life in a new town: good relationships at work, the support and friendship of other Christians and recreation outside both. If all three don't fall into your lap straight away, remember that tea that brews slowly tastes better in the long run.

alan macdonald

''Then start to hunt in the local newspaper...''

The good church guide

Finding the right church or fellowship for you isn't always easy. Especially if you see yourself as a comparison shopper looking for the perfect church. It doesn't exist.

One thing to look for, however, is a genuine desire by the church or fellowship to follow biblical teaching. In the same way that this is the desire of a Christian (see 1 Peter 1:23-25), so it should be that of the church.

(Titus 1:9, Revelation 3:1,3)

After that the desirable qualities are many and varied – good preaching, biblical worship, friendliness, evangelism, good works, good order and a joy in Christ. You won't find all of these but they're something to look for.

Cast your eyes down the job ads column:

'Ambitious self-starter needed for key position ...'

'We are the market leaders ....'

'A real career opportunity awaits

you ...'

'Energetic and motivated school leavers wanted ...'

'Dull, routine job offers below average salary ...'

Wait a minute,

WHAT IF I DON'T LAND THE PERFECT JOB?

job ads like that never appear in the newspaper columns. If advertisements really reflected the jobs that are offered we might never apply. Routine jobs are far more numerous than the openings for ambitious, determined, creative, executive material. Many of us believe that if we study hard enough, get together the right CV, write enough letters (oh, and pray often enough), we'll eventually land the perfect job.

But what if we don't? What if the job we land turns out to be a disappointment? What if it fails to utilize the talents and abilities we are bursting to use? Even worse, what if I don't find a job at all? What if I'm left unemployed for months or even longer? God wouldn't let that happen, would he? Surely he wants the best for me, so he will get me the best job?

These are important questions since their answers underlie my whole search for a career in my life. Could God allow me to be unemployed or to take up a job that didn't really use my abilities? Reassuring Bible verses spring to mind, 'Have life and have it to the full' and 'In all things God works for the good of those who love him.'

(John 10:10)
(Romans 8:32)

These passages rightly remind us that God really does want the best for our lives. Yet there is no specific mention of our *career prosperity* being assured. In fact the Bible contains some disturbing examples in the lives of some of God's most faithful children. Job was one of the most prosperous businessmen of his time, yet he was allowed to lose it all. David was a successful soldier, but was forced to live as a refugee for a time as a result of his success. Paul was a highly respected Pharisee, but endured poverty, prison and homelessness when he became an apostle.

'This doesn't sound like the sort of success I have in mind!'

Following Christ doesn't guarantee a smooth path to career fulfilment. For Matthew, the tax collector, and Luke, the doctor, leaving everything to follow a penniless Messiah was not a good career move.

> "Jesus hides nothing on the job description he offers us ..."

Jesus hides nothing on the job description he offers us, 'If anyone would come after me, he must deny himself and take up his cross.' This means that whatever our career hopes and

(Matthew 16:24)

aspirations, we have to put them second to God's will for us. If we are only following Jesus along the routes we want to go, it is more likely that we're only following our ambitions.

We cannot assume then that God will not lead Christians into unemployment or difficult and frustrating jobs. These situations will not be the norm or the ideal. Nevertheless at some point in our lives there may be things God wants to teach us through the rough ride rather than the smooth.

*f*our lessons to be learned from career frustration

"What do you do?"

1. The real source of our self-worth. This can so easily be in our career. On first acquaintance one of the opening questions people ask is: 'What do you do?' If you answer, 'I'm on the dustcarts', they may look at you in disbelief. If you reply, 'Well, I haven't got a job at the moment ...', often you are met with embarrassed silence. The source of embarrassment is that they don't know how to proceed with the conversation from there. We like to be able to put people in boxes labelled 'lawyer', 'computer analyst', 'builder', 'teacher'. If somebody can't offer us a label then we are unsure how to relate to them.

This practice underlines just how much of our self-worth is invested in our jobs. To experience unemployment or low-grade work is to find ourselves apologizing for not fitting in with the box mentality. We may soon find that we start to question our own self-worth because of others' attitudes.

The good news is that God is not going to ask you what job you did when you get to heaven. His priorities are utterly different from ours.

THE PERFECT JOB?

'What does the Lord require of you? To act justly and to love mercy and to walk humbly with your God.' There are no redundant people in God's kingdom. We are all given the same work when we enter. Our work is to foster a loving relationship with our God and with our neighbours. Thankfully, doing this is in no way dependent on having a successful job.

(Micah 6:8)

2. Identifying with the oppressed. There may even be times when it is a positive advantage not to have a successful well paid job. The advantages may not seem obvious to us, but we have to remember that God is no respecter of persons. He is as concerned about the housewife or the out of work labourer as he is about the business executive.

Try witnessing to a road sweeper or someone in the dole queue whilst wearing an office suit and tie. They will be suspicious of you. They have a right to, since you are telling them about a better life from a position of obvious material advantage. Only Christians who know what it is to be out of work and undervalued by society can talk in practical terms about God's saving grace to those in the same position.

The same applies to a humdrum and unexciting job. You may be wondering what on earth God is doing letting you stagnate in such a backwater. At the same time the person next to you may be wondering what you can talk about to get you through the day. If God never let Christians take humdrum jobs, a high percentage of the population would never hear about Christ.

3. God's upside-down values. We are apt to put a value on an occupation by the money someone is prepared to pay for it to be done. By this

"God doesn't pay by the hour ..."

definition the apostle Paul wasted most of his life.

God doesn't pay by the hour, nor does he judge our work by what it's worth on the open market. It is so easy to feel a second class citizen because we 'only' do voluntary work, look after children or help part-time in an old people's home. These are the very things that God values most. As Christians we must keep the upside-down values of the kingdom firmly in our sights. Having a fat wallet or status in society is easy to desire, but both are passing glories. Building God's kingdom is storing up eternal treasures.

(James 1:27)

4. Waiting is good for you. There have been times when I would have screamed if someone had said this to me. But looking back I have to admit it can be true. Praising God with promotion just round the corner isn't difficult. Doing it when the right job never seems to materialize is hard, but is the real essence of faith. 'Faith is being sure of what we hope for and certain of what we do not see.'

" ... the real essence of faith ..."

(Hebrews 11:1)

Perhaps hoping for the perfect job to come along will always be an illusion since the perfect job does not exist. By 'hope' the Bible means a strong-rooted conviction. This can never be grounded in the ups and downs of the career market, only in the character of God himself. Whatever we go through his Father-love is working for our ultimate and eternal good.

alan macdonald